Integration or Segregation for the Physically Handicapped Child?

Integration or Segregation for the Physically Handicapped Child?

By

SUSAN SCHMIDT DIBNER, Ph.D.

*Post-Doctoral Sociology Research Fellow, Duke University Center
for the Study of Aging and Human Development*

and

ANDREW S. DIBNER, Ph.D.

*Associate Professor of Psychology, Boston University
Research Consultant, Massachusetts Easter Seal Society
Senior Research Fellow, Duke University Center
for the Study of Aging and Human Development*

CHARLES C THOMAS • PUBLISHER
Springfield • Illinois • U.S.A.

Published and Distributed Throughout the World by

CHARLES C THOMAS • PUBLISHER

Bannerstone House

301-327 East Lawrence Avenue, Springfield, Illinois, U.S.A.

©*1973, by* CHARLES C THOMAS • PUBLISHER

ISBN 0-398-02817-6

Library of Congress Catalog Card Number: 73-233

*With THOMAS BOOKS careful attention is given to all details of
manufacturing and design. It is the Publisher's desire to present books that are
satisfactory as to their physical qualities and artistic possibilities and
appropriate for their particular use. THOMAS BOOKS will be true to those
laws of quality that assure a good name and good will.*

Printed in the United States of America
N-1

To
MILTON HENRY SCHMIDT
1901 - 1968

PREFACE AND ACKNOWLEDGMENTS

THIS book took the first breath of its life when Dick LaPierre of the Massachusetts Easter Seal Society asked the hard question: "Are we really doing the right thing, sending our handicapped children to normal summer camps?" The Society had made that decision to guide its big camping program, with the conviction that handicapped children had to learn how to grow up in a normal world.

The camping program was successful. By the end of each summer, the Society received quite a few grateful letters from parents and campers. But beyond anecdotes from Camp Directors, and glimpses from brief camp visits, mostly for trouble-shooting, Dick knew they really did not know enough about the program to justify long range planning. We were asked to do this study.

To us the question of handicapped children in different settings took on much of the complexity and excitement of the big social science issue of our time: the influence of the environment on the individual and his behavior. We were both very much for the trend in social science from the search for constancies in the individual to the conception that a person's behavior is only meaningful in terms of the setting he is in.

While the study progressed we got absorbed by the jarring problem of conflicting values which inhabit the American mind. "Everyone is an individual," but "Treat everyone the same." "Be normal," but "Fight to win."

Where can the "different" person fit in? Imagine you are up close to a person with a severe physical deformity. "Don't stare," you tell yourself, though you want desparately to stare and stare until you understand and stop feeling that awful combination of feelings: fascination? horror? pity? Remember, treat him *the same*, though he is not the same.

The social issues surrounding the physical handicapped child were so obviously like other social issues of our day. Could we have something general to say about integration and segregation? Could we propose solutions to racial conflicts? No, we could not. Not now. Not until the concepts we found to be helpful in understanding our problem might be thought through in relation to other situations of minority-majority conflict and tested with larger samples than represented here.

We wanted to make our thoughts available to as large an audience as possible, and so we avoided scientific jargon. We are hopeful that many may learn from our experience: planners of services for handicapped children, therapists, educators, recreation specialists, and parents, as well as social scientists.

Many people have contributed to the study, both directly and indirectly, and they have our deepest respect and gratitude. The Easter Seal Society for Crippled Children and Adults of Massachusetts was the parent of the study, providing support, facilities, contacts and spirit. We are especially thankful to its Executive Director, Richard LaPierre and to Ted Kershaw, Joan Turner, Dorothy Jeffries, Ruth Thompson, Don Perry and Art Miller. With the sponsorship of the Massachusetts Society and Boston University (thanks to Joseph Speisman and Philip Kubzansky) we were supported for two years by a grant from the Easter Seal Research Foundation (No. R6918) for which we are grateful.

The study could not have been accomplished without the generous cooperation of camp directors, counselors and campers. Among those to whom we are most indebted are Bernice Leslie, William Haney, Gregg Ouellette, and Don Perry. The campers and counselors are too numerous to name but they all earned our admiration and thanks.

Many students at Boston University assisted at various stages of the project and we remember their help with gratitude: Joan Huser, Kay Horowitz, Martha Greenberg, Lee Kalmanson, Nancy Ehrlich and Michael Feuerstein.

Our greatest help came from some of our teachers, colleagues or seminal writers whose insights into human behavior have strongly influenced us. We are especially grateful to Tamara Dembo, Erving Goffman, Everett Hughes, Kurt Lewin, Robert S. Weiss, and

Beatrice Wright.

Susan would also like to thank the readers of her doctoral dissertation at Brandeis University: Rosabeth Kanter, Gordon Fellman, Maurice Schwartz and Irving Zola.

SUSAN SCHMIDT DIBNER
ANDREW S. DIBNER

CONTENTS

Integration or Segregation for the Physically Handicapped Child?

Chapter One

oooooooooooooooooooooooooooooooooooooooo

WHICH WORLD TO LIVE IN?

oooooooooooooooooooooooooooooooooooooooo

THE physically handicapped person in our culture which stresses physical beauty and functional efficiency is a deviant. The physically handicapped are stigmatized, pitied, derided, ignored, patronized and reacted to with solicitude and controlled behavior. Normal persons often have conflicting feelings when with a blind or deaf person, someone in a wheelchair, or severely obese. They may be repulsed by the physical deformity while at the same time they feel pity and fascination. They may be angry or threatened by a physical handicap while simultaneously feeling guilty for these negative reactions. It is not unusual for normal persons to hesitate in making any contact at all with the handicapped for fear their negative feelings will be revealed.

It is permissible in our society to openly express negative reactions to prostitutes, drug addicts or delinquents. The implication is that such deviants have willingly brought on their difficulties. They have behaved badly and therefore may be treated badly. The same is not true of such other "inferior" groups as the aged, women or physically handicapped people. Society's message is quite clear: it is wrong to treat them badly. Afterall, their unfortunate condition is not brought about by errant behavior. They are innocent of misdeed. "There but for the grace of God go I."

MANAGEMENT TECHNIQUES

To relieve much of this tension generated between the physically handicapped and non-handicapped, social *management techniques* are often employed. The handicapped individual learns

3

techniques for dealing with a world made for normals with its physical requirements, temporal pacing and social expectations all geared to those possessing the average range of abilities. The pressure on them is to appear as normal as possible so that they will not invoke feelings of pity, anger or repulsion and thus be accepted by others. Management techniques help in achieving this semblance of normalcy.

Normal persons, in turn, learn to manage their interaction by overlooking physical deviations and, as far as possible, treat handicapped people as if their disability does not exist. It has been well documented, however, that while management techniques help in smoothing the interaction between normal and handicapped individuals, the social acceptance this leads to is actually only a conditional one. That is, the handicapped individual will be treated as normal and accepted as long as he or she manages to maintain a relative appearance of normalcy, withdrawing from those types of interaction where the handicap would be obvious or disruptive.

TO SEGREGATE OR INTEGRATE?

Some formal and informal institutions in our society have been established to help the handicapped person face these problems. The government promotes hiring of the handicapped, schools hire special teachers, community agencies provide counseling services or recreational opportunities. In recent years there has been an increase in the self-help movement, where deviants gather together for mutual support, pooling of resources and building of political power.

Notable among these have been the success of Alcoholics Anonymous, Golden Age Clubs and the Association for Aid to Retarded Children. The self-help groups are examples of self-segregation of persons who feel that because of their differentness they are unable to achieve satisfaction of their needs in the majority group and seek it among *their own*. Now we see a growing number of women's groups signaling the rising consciousness by women of their discriminated status in American society.

An underlying issue is whether it is better to segregate or

integrate those who are different. To what extent should they be grouped with others of their own kind? There is also the question as to which group an individual selects for himself or herself.

As Robert Scott (1969) points out, there are agencies devoted to helping the blind which support segregation by setting up special programs and activities which cater to the specific needs of those without sight. They may create a dependency on the part of a handicapped person on the agency which then acts to keep that person segregated.

For the blind, there are agencies which create a comfortable world for those without sight and encourage clients to look for enjoyment and social contacts within it. Elevators have braille push buttons, bingo is played with braille cards and assistants help and praise members of the group for each accomplishment. Other agencies do not emphasize the segregated, sheltering atmosphere. They work toward keeping individuals within a community despite the discomfort and isolation which might result.

Despite good intentions, social agencies may be teaching the social role of being blind rather than facilitating maximal functional ability. The emphasis is upon appearing as normal as possible in order to gain social acceptance by those who do not have a handicap.

The use of cosmetic prostheses pinpoints the conflict between these diverse goals. A disabled person who has only a partial arm must decide whether wearing a cosmetic arm prosthesis which makes him look normal but which may cut down efficiency is preferable. If so, under what conditions? While one choice might lead to quicker or fuller social acceptance because the arm now *looks right* and will not offend, the other solution may result in being able to do more things.

By surrounding oneself with people who are similarly handicapped, a person with such a disability as the partial arm described above may be freer to drop the normal appearing behavior. In a segregated group he may not be confronted with the dilemma of whether it is better to wear a cosmetic arm or not. But he must then ask, what price freedom? What are the psychological consequences of being segregated? Can he or she get along in the real world?

THE QUESTION FOR CHILDREN

These questions have been often debated among society's planners in relation to deviant children. There seem to be several reasons for this concern with children. First, a child's life is more subject to planned and prescribed activities than that of adults. Second, with children still in the process of being socialized, there is the feeling that they have more potential for change and improvement.

In discussing education for the deviant child, some scholars and practitioners advocate segregated schools or special classes which can be geared to the specific needs of the youngsters. It is argued that special classes can provide more care for physical needs and fairer competition. Since normal children are not present, special equipment or learning tools can be used to accommodate those needing additional help to learn.

It is also believed by some that deviant children (the physically handicapped, mentally retarded, or socially impoverished) will adversely affect or retard the learning process of the non-deviant child if integrated into the same group. According to Blackman and Heintz (1966), in their review of the literature concerning the placement of the mentally retarded in regular or special schools, there have been two distinct trends in the placement controversy. Those favoring integration of the retarded into regular classes argue that the close proximity to normal peers helps the retarded academically and socially, as well as being more democratic. Proponents of special schools argue that better services can be provided in controlled settings. In addition the reduction of competition and fear of failure that would be found in the regular classes would promote better emotional adjustment.

The basic issues underlying these debates concern fair competition for the handicapped youngster, the development of optimum academic and physical achievement, and the achievement of a good social and psychological adjustment. The question is not whether these goals are important for the developing child with or without a physical handicap, but how they can best be achieved. The debate revolves around the question whether it is better to segregate or integrate children with handicaps. Does a child with a handicap stand a better chance of learning more in a sheltered setting where special equipment and staff can be employed, or integrated into a non-special setting where non-handicapped children can contribute to the learning process of those with a disability?

What about a child's self concept or psychological adjustment? Is this likely to be more positive if the child does not have to face competition with non-handicapped youngsters, or is self-esteem enhanced by meeting the challenge of the normal world?

If a child is segregated in school or camp, does this make it impossible for him or her to adjust to the real world later on? These are some of the questions which will be discussed in this study. The focus here is on physically handicapped children, some of whom attended regular summer camps and others a special camp for crippled children. Our purpose was to examine the social structures of these integrated and segregated settings and try to explore their effects on the social behavior, relationships, feelings and attitudes of children and camp staff. By this means, we might derive some of the limitations and assets of integration and segregation.

While society's planners may establish or promote segregation over integration or integration over segregation, for the best development of the physically handicapped child it is ultimately the parents who make this decision. It is interesting to see how attitudes of parents of handicapped children reflect the conflict between segregation and integration.

A questionnaire was sent to 150 parents of handicapped children attending camps in the Summer of 1968. Half the children attended a special camp, half attended a regular camp which accepted some children with disabilities.

Eighty-one percent of the parents with children in a segregated camp, stated that they felt it was better for a handicapped child to be segregated. They felt that the competition was fairer, their children would form a better self-concept away from competition and attitudes of non-handicapped children. The parents also thought that they would learn more through the use of special equipment and personnel.

On the other hand, 88 percent of the parents whose child

attended an integrated camp felt their child would fare better in the integrated setting. To them, integration promoted better self-concepts, competition and social and psychological development (Dibner and Dibner, 1971).

Parents' reasons for preferring opposite type camps were often the same. Some parents saw their child learning to cope with his handicap in a regular camp, others in a segregated camp. Some thought competition could best be sought with normal children, others with handicapped children in a sheltered setting. The same was true of parents' concern for their child being made to feel different. Some felt this would occur through his being segregated whereas others feared the rejection and teasing of normal children.

It is important to examine integration and segregation from the perspective of what is best for the child. It is also important to look at it from the perspective of planning and actual administration of a camp, school or class which serves only children with a handicap or strives to program for children who have handicaps and others who are normal.

What are some of the conflicts a teacher or counselor in a camp must face when leading group activities for children whose functional abilities vary greatly or whose pace varies from extremely slow to quite fast? How can such conflicts be resolved? What are the consequences of asking the more competent children to slow themselves down to accommodate the more disabled youngsters? Counselors and administrative staff members dealt with these issues daily in both the segregated and integrated camps and a better understanding of what problems they had and what was done to resolve them takes us a step further in understanding the contributions or limitations of integration and segregation.

TERMINOLOGY

Throughout this study the terms *normal, handicapped, non-handicapped, disabled, non-disabled,* and *deviant* are used to describe the children attending camps. It is important to discuss some implications in the use of these terms for they carry with them assumptions and value judgments which reflect upon the meaning of the data presented.

Handicapped and Non-handicapped

It is difficult to choose an appropriate term which can be used with comfort in describing the children in this study. Handicapped and non-handicapped are inadequate terms because they infer that there are two groups of children at opposite extremes of one another. This is not the case, for it is not clear where the line is to be drawn between being handicapped or non-handicapped. Some of the youngsters who were considered handicapped because they were Easter Seal campers may have been less handicapped than others called normal. One must consider in what areas of functioning a person is limited, as well as in what social situation the action is taking place.

Webster's *New World Dictionary* (1961) defines handicapped as "something that hinders a person; impedes. . . ." It is far from clear which children attending camp were hindered and which were not. While some could not perform well in physical activities, they were successful in games of verbal skills or interaction requiring strong personality traits. Likewise, while some children were skilled in physical performances, they were handicapped emotionally or intellectually within their specific group placements. Perhaps there can be no term applicable across the board since being hindered depends upon the fit between social setting and individual characteristics.

Disabled

Beatrice Wright chose to use the term disability rather than handicap, pointing out the distinction between the terms made by K. W. Hamilton:

> A disability is a condition of impairment physical or mental, having an objective aspect that can usually be described by a physician. . . . A handicap is the cumulative result of the obstacles which disability interposes between the individual and his maximum functional level. (Wright, 1960)

This definition hinges on an objective measure or state which can be delineated by a physician. However, not all conditions medically described are handicaps. As Wright (1960) illustrates,

Chinese ladies bound their feet but this did not impair their functional ability since they were not required to be efficiently mobile. A person may feel physically handicapped even though his limitations have no medical labeling. A woman walking alone at night may feel physically limited if approached by a man.

There is no clear demarcation between who is physically disabled and who is not. Once a physical characteristic becomes an impairment, should it be considered a handicap? Are the aged physically handicapped once their functioning is impaired although this is not necessarily a medically described state? Such issues are not easily answered and make it difficult to be concise in terminology.

It is interesting to note that when asked if they had any physical handicaps, 2/3 of male cabin counselors at the segregated camp said that they did, mentioning among other handicaps "not living up to my potential in school," or "mumbling because of shyness." Only one female cabin counselor answered that she had any handicap: her temper. Attitude towards one's ability to function plays a part in determining whether one has or does not have a handicap or disability.

Deviant

Jonathan Freedman and Anthony Doob in their work, *Deviancy: The Psychology of Being Different* (1968) employ the term deviant. They clearly define what they mean by this state. Dropping previous uses of the term which included negative attitudes by others, criminal or anti-social acts or non-compliance to group norms, they consider deviancy as a *feeling* on the part of the individual so labeled. "Whenever one is different from the rest of the group he is in, he is at least for that moment a deviant. . . ." (Freedman and Doob, 1968, p. 3).

The term deviant in this sense is applicable to the present study, although, as implied, who is deviant can change from moment to moment and from situation to situation. It may not be a child who has a physical handicap who feels deviant. In the segregated camp, staff members' children who were in the program were deviant at that camp because they did not have a physical disability. They were too physically able for this setting. Deviancy as used in the present study reflects also the fit between the social situation and actors within it.

Terms Used in Present Study

We will generally use the terms handicapped and non-handicapped children. Children who are called handicapped in this study have several things in common. All of their applications to camp were made through an Easter Seal Society. Parents and Easter Seal Society personnel considered these youngsters handicapped and they were part of a special camping program. They all possessed a medically defined disability.

It is likely that some youngsters in the non-handicapped category also had one or another medically defined limitation but they were not seen as *special* campers by camp staff and they were not part of the group of handicapped campers. Although each handicapped child was identified as disabled and in need of special help by his parents and the Easter Seal agency, it is always a question in each individual case as to whether a child considers himself or herself as different. All names of camps, campers and staff have been changed.

Chapter Two

~~~~~~

WHO TO STUDY AND HOW?

~~~~~~

Our opportunity to explore the social and psychological effects of integrative and segregative social structures came through the interest of the Massachusetts Easter Seal Society in evaluating their extensive camping program for handicapped children. The summer camp program was one of the largest of their many service programs for the handicapped, and they had taken a definite stance in a controversial area. They resisted the idea of a heavy investment in operating a special camp for handicapped children, and instead were pioneering in promoting their assignment to regular camps.

Over a period of several years, they had established cooperative relationships with 123 residential and day camps to which they were annually sending more than 200 children. They were continually developing methods of screening and assigning children to camps, methods of orienting counselors, and techniques for coping with the myriad problems of transportation, special health care, diets and so forth.

For the more severely disabled children who could not possibly participate in a regular camp program, the society was experimenting with *special units* in a regular camp. This was a cabin of handicapped children and special counselors. There were programs arranged just for this group as well as some joint activities with normal campers. Underlying the Society's committment to integrated camping was the belief that handicapped children would best learn to adjust to the normal world by experiencing the normal world.

To help the Society decide if their approach was the most fruitful one, we conducted a series of studies, making observations in several of the cooperating camps, interviewing campers, staff and directors, and sending questionnaires to hundreds of handicapped and non-handicapped campers and their parents. These early studies of the Society's integrated camping program concluded that a handicapped child's adjustment to camp was not so much related to his previous experience in camping or the type of disability he had, as it was to his social maturity, and the degree to which his disability permitted him to participate in the particular activities valued by the group to which he was assigned.

Counselor reports on those children rated poorly adjusted showed that their handicap interfered with activities. Reports on better adjusted campers showed that they participated in more activities (Dibner & Dibner, 1968).

The social structure of the camp seemed to be a central factor influencing the type of adjustment likely for a handicapped child. A camp's social structure is its complex system of role relationships. It determines to a large extent which other campers and counselors a child may come in contact with, and the circumstances and atmosphere in which the interactions will occur. A camp's social structure is affected by its goals in camping, physical facilities and terrain, cabin, age or other groupings, programming, and general rules about freedom of movement and communication within the camp.

An intensive field study was proposed as the best way to explore the relationships between integrative and segregative social structures and their social-psychological effects on campers.

Since field studies are very costly in time, and we could study only a limited few, we selected Camp Cherokee (for boys) and Camp Hiawatha (for girls) from those integrated camps used by the Massachusetts Easter Seal Society, and Camp Woodland, run by the Easter Seal Society of a neighboring state as representative of segregated camps.

Camp Cherokee and Hiawatha met our criteria for selection. They were representative of other regular camps used by the Easter Seal Society for the placement of handicapped children; they had previous experience with handicapped youngsters so that integration of normal and disabled youngsters was not a new experience for them; and personnel of both camps were favorable to our research plans involving the use of their camps and interviewing of campers and staff.

A boys' camp and a girls' camp had to be selected because there were no coeducational camps in the Society's program. Both were average sized camps, though the session we studied Camp Hiawatha it was not completely filled. Both were located in rural areas, and served campers of approximately the same socio-economic class. These two camps were scheduled to have five handicapped children per session, a richer source of observational data than many other camps which had a smaller number of Easter Seal campers integrated into their programs.

Camps Hiawatha and Cherokee were both highly regarded by the Easter Seal Society personnel as giving a good camping experience for referred children. Criteria for the selection of Camp Woodland were similar to those followed in choosing the integrated camps, although it was necessary to work through another state's Easter Seal Society, since the Massachusetts Society did not operate a special camp.

Camp Woodland was known to be a successful state agency camp for handicapped children and representative of other state-supported segregated camps. It was comparable to the integrated camps chosen in terms of being agency-supported, the children were approximately of the same social class, and programs at all three camps were comparable. The camp staff was also interested and cooperative.

TIMETABLE

In June 1969 the authors moved to a cabin near Camp Hiawatha (for girls) a week before the opening two week session. Field research was conducted at this location for three weeks: one week of counselor orientation and pre-camp activity, and two weeks to cover a complete camper session.

Camp Cherokee (for boys) opened later than Camp Hiawatha, so we were able to spend three weeks at the boys' camp: one week during counselor orientation and two weeks of the opening session for campers. Again we rented a small cabin near the camp for easy access during all times of the day and week.

At Camp Woodland, the segregated coeducational camp, data

was collected for five weeks in the summer of 1970: one week of counselor orientation and four weeks representing the complete first session for campers.

FIELD OBSERVATIONS

Observations were made at varying times of the day and night. We sampled behavior from the time children awoke to the time they went to sleep. Cabin activities, formal and informal play, feeding, rest periods, outings, crafts, water activities, and evening programs were all observed.

At times focus was on cabin groups, a clique, an activities group or work group. At other times it was upon an individual camper or counselor working together or alone. The most important criterion for deciding which group to observe at which time was whether or not the group included handicapped campers.

Some observations were made of normal campers (or groups) without handicapped campers present but these were limited in number. Of main concern in the observations was the interaction which occurred between campers, whether handicapped or not, and the staff members.

Periods of observations usually lasted one to two hours after which the researcher would retreat to a private place to tape record his or her observations. Notes were not taken in the field except in instances where detailed movements were of interest. Usually after recording observations, the researcher would return to the camp. When one researcher was recording, the other remained at the camp so that it was covered most of the day.

SELECTION OF SUBJECTS FOR INTERVIEWING

Integrated Camps

Table I summarizes the number of campers interviewed for the field study. In the integrated situation all handicapped campers were formally interviewed. Five were in attendance at each of the integrated camps, representing different ages, types of physical disabilities and range of mental functioning and cultural

TABLE I

CAMPERS, COUNSELORS AND STAFF OBSERVED AND INTERVIEWED

| | Integrated Camps | | | | Segregated Camp | |
| | Hiawatha (girls) | | Cherokee (boys) | | Woodland (boys and girls) | |
	Obs.	Int.	Obs.	Int.	Obs.	Int.
Campers:						
Non-Handicapped	60	15	118	12	–	–
Handicapped	5	5	5	5	96	36
Total	65	20	123	17	96	36
Counselors & Staff:	18	7	32	14	52	34

backgrounds. (See Chapters 3 and 4 for further details on demographic background of campers in the study.)

For each handicapped child, two normal children were selected as control subjects. These non-disabled campers were chosen from the same cabin group as the subjects and were selected on the basis of being of similar age, race, and socio-economic background.

Agreement as to which normal children would be control subjects was reached by the two researchers who based their judgement upon discussion with cabin counselors and camp directors, and with consultation of the camper application forms. The control subjects selected were meant to be as representative of the 8 to 10 normal children in the entire cabin group as possible.

In addition to the control group of campers, a number of additional children were questioned. This latter group was selected to represent the entire camp body, including honor campers or those with discipline problems. When two handicapped children were placed in the same cabin, all cabin members were interviewed so that there would be complete information on one cabin group per camp. In all, 27 non-handicapped boys and girls were interviewed to compare with the 10 handicapped children in the integrated camps.

All staff members who had handicapped youngsters in their

charge were interviewed, especially cabin counselors. Special staff such as the waterfront directors and the craft counselors were interviewed for they worked with the handicapped campers also. Camp directors were interviewed on a formal and informal basis.

Segregated Camp

In this camp all children were handicapped and we were faced with the problem of how to select a sample for intensive study. Those selected to be observed and interviewed most closely were chosen after a week of observation by agreement between the two researchers in conjunction with camp personnel. The 36 children included in the study were selected on the following criteria:

1. That they be comparable to those studied in the integrated camps in terms of age, sex, socio-economic status, type and degree of disability. Focus was upon those youngsters who could have been placed in an integrated camp had they applied to another Easter Seal Society.

2. That they be comparable to children studied previously in terms of mental functioning. Policy among the three camps varied in regard to the acceptance of youngsters with mental retardation.

To supplement the first group of children selected for study outlined above, additional children were included in the study so that the group of campers attending a segregated camp as a whole would be represented. We wanted to include the following dimensions of disability:

1. *Hidden handicaps:* whereby others may or may not have been aware that a child was handicapped, or if so in what way handicapped.

2. *Acquired at birth or in later years:* a fact which may affect interaction since individual may vary in how they deal with others if they have had the experience of having been normal themselves.

3. *Varying in type:* sensory, verbal or motor skills which affect different areas of interaction.

4. *Varying in degree of severity:* representing all degrees of functional

ability and dependency on others.

The 36 children interviewed in the segregated camp included 19 boys and 17 girls. Three out of four counselors from each cabin were interviewed, as well as staff members involved in leading activities or providing therapy. (See Chapters 3 and 4 for further details on children and counselors included in the study.)

INTERVIEWS

Interviews with campers and counselors were semi-structured and tape recorded, and took approximately 45 minutes to an hour. On sunny days, interviews were conducted outside in secluded areas selected to insure privacy with little distraction for the respondent. On rainy days interviews were held in otherwise empty camp buildings.

Interviews for campers were designed to cover the following areas:

1. Demographic information
2. Friendship networks
3. Attitude toward camp and staff
4. Feelings of competence.

At the end of the interview, each child was given a short self concept test which is described in Chapter Eleven. All interview schedules appear in the Appendix.

Interviews for counselors and staff covered the following areas:

1. Demographic information
2. Past work experience and future occupational plans
3. Attitude toward handicapped children, handicapped and non-handicapped campers
4. Problems encountered in work at camp
5. Attitude toward camp and camping.

GROUP DISCUSSIONS

Camp personnel were aware of our interest in handicapped and non-handicapped camper interaction and were asked to meet with us once or twice during the two weeks' time for group discussions concerning their work. These discussions were open to free exchange on all aspects of camp life affecting the handicapped campers and were also tape recorded. They served as another rich source of data and helped greatly in the good rapport between the researchers and counselor staff.

THE RESEARCHERS: A HUSBAND AND WIFE TEAM

The fact that there were two researchers, one man and one woman, well suited the situations being studied. It was possible for at least one researcher to be present in any situation: going to bed, changing clothes to go swimming, accompanying children on an overnight hike. At each camp, one researcher could continue field observations under circumstances at which the other would not have been welcomed.

When there are two, there is likely to be a difference of opinion. Many times we approached an incident with different perspectives and through seemingly endless discussions came to understand what we were observing in greater depth. At times we were both present for the same activity and could later compare and discuss fieldnotes. At other times one would observe an activity group, while the other might be observing at the waterfront.

We were usually introduced to the campers by the Camp Director the first day of camp, usually in the dining hall during announcements after the noon meal. They were told that we were writing a book on camping. In the main, campers were more than eager to talk with us about themselves and the camp. Near the end of the two week session when formal interviewing began, more children than we could talk to were asking to be included in the interviews.

At Camp Hiawatha, the girls enjoyed the fact that we were married and seemed to take delight in kidding us about it. Some girls related to us as parents (often those from broken homes). By the end of the two week session, we had become camp mascots; people who were invited to join specific camp events or sought after to tell secrets.

But at Camp Cherokee, we were not often perceived as a couple. Because the older boys were to leave camp early in their stay to go on the overnight trip, we split up. Susan covered the three younger boy villages while Andrew observed and interviewed the older boys. We were rarely seen together in that camp.

Similarly, at Woodland Camp we were not often together. The boys' and girls' living areas were separated from one another and members of the opposite sex were not allowed in the others' area. For this reason, we spent most of our time with children of the same sex. Although we were known to others, there was little cross-sex identification with the researchers. On the other hand, with children of the same sex, the researchers were sought after as a friend or confidant by many campers.

Considerable effort was made to acquaint the camp directors and staff with the purpose of the research, methods to be used, and the background and training of the researchers. We were sensitive to the discomfort on the part of some staff members to being observed and tried to openly recognize it as much as possible. It was brought up for group discussion in all camps.

Almost all counselors expressed positive feelings toward the research and in most cases, anxiety about being observed receded after a few days. Some counselors were intellectually curious about the study and some identified themselves as future researchers. A few staff members remained guarded throughout.

PARTICIPANT OBSERVATION VERSUS NON-PARTICIPANT OBSERVATION

There was always the question of the degree of participation in the camp life which had to be faced. Any participation by observers influences the event being observed. On the other hand, complete uninvolvement can be perceived by participants as antisocial behavior, which could in turn influence events negatively.

We found that a minimal amount of low-keyed participation was best. For example, during swimming, observations were made of those in the water while chatting with one or two youngsters who were lounging on shore. On occasion when the researchers were asked to join in an activity, they would do so rather than repeatedly refuse. We almost always ate at campers' tables rather than the staff tables to be closer to the social interaction of the campers.

When campers sought the help of the researchers with a personal problem, while an ear would be given, such problems were redirected to someone within the camp hierarchy.

An incident which occurred while we were collecting data at Camp Woodland might best serve to illustrate how we worked together and benefited from the fact that there were two of us.

Near the end of two weeks of the camp session at the segregated camp we were interviewing cabin counselors, Andrew talking to the male staff and Susan the female staff. Back at our cabin one night while discussing some of the responses together, we came across an interesting difference in answers between the male and female counselors. While the boys usually answered "yes" to the question, "Do you have a handicap yourself?", the girls were universally saying "no."

We discussed this difference and made several guesses as to why we might be getting such a discrepancy. It was finally decided that we were asking the question differently, therefore evoking different answers.

Going back to the tapes of the original interviews, we listened to each other speaking and then decided to probe harder and wait longer before asking the next question, even if there was only silence.

After changing the way in which the words of the question were emphasized, we compared notes once again. The difference between sexes remained. After checking the fact against other data collected, we decided that we had a true sex difference in response to this question; a fact that could later be incorporated into the data analysis with confidence.

Chapter Three

WOODLAND, A SEGREGATED CAMP

W HILE driving down the mile-long dirt road through thick woods to Woodland Camp, one is greeted by a series of welcome signs. Crudely hand-painted signs nailed to trees say: "Welcome"; "We're glad you're here", "We say hello." There are many visitors to this camp designed for handicapped children: parents, health-field workers, fund raisers and donors, well-meaning members of charity groups, as well as reporters from local news media.

The camp session is composed of two 4-week periods separated by a week's break in which all children and counselors leave. Approximately 80 percent of the children attend both sessions.

The camp is situated on a large lake which can be seen from all points of the camp. Although the Easter Seal Society which sponsors Camp Woodland owns a large acreage, the actual area which each child must cover in his or her daily activities is relatively small. New modern cabins are close together, lined up along the banks of the lake.

The camp is coeducational. Three girls' cabins are to the right of the main dining hall and centrally located athletic field and swimming area. Three boys' cabins are to the left. Boys and girls are not allowed to go into each others area except for special occasions.

Five new cabins and one older building house the six camper groups. Each cabin sleeps from sixteen to eighteen youngsters in addition to four to five counselors who have a separate living area in the center of each building. A large fireplace located in front of a picture window overlooks the lake and serves two purposes. It provides heat on cold, rainy days and it provides a home-like atmosphere or livingroom area for the cabin members. Evening activities are often games and stories told in front of the fireplace.

The camp is designed to eliminate architectural barriers for the handicapped person. There are no double bunks; each youngster has a single cot surrounded by ample space for wheelchairs or storing of braces. Campers' cots are arranged around the outer walls of the cabin and partial wall dividers section off two beds. Children refer to bunkmates who share these cubicles.

Each cabin has several toilets, a shower and sinks, all with grab bars. There are no doors or thresholds. Blacktop paths run from the cabin areas to the athletic area, dining hall, therapy and crafts buildings, all of which can be entered by ramp or stairs. Children eat in cabin groups at large tables. Counselors and kitchen girls serve food from a kitchen adjoining the eating area.

As with the cabins, the dining hall also looks out onto the lake. A large grassy area in front of this building is used for athletics and runs down to a sandy beach and swimming area. There is a wooden ramp at the swimming area used to roll wheelchairs down to the water where children are lifted and carried in. The camp owns canoes and rowboats, as well as a specially built pontoon boat designed to carry eight children in wheelchairs.

Swimming is considered one of the most important programs offered. Children have instructional swim and free swims daily. There are three pool areas, the largest being shallow enough for children to support themselves on their arms if necessary. In addition to the water sports, the camp program also offers crafts, dramatics, athletics, camp craft and nature.

These regular activities are supplemented by special events. At times outsiders come to Camp Woodland with rock bands or other forms of entertainment. Each summer Shriners arrive with many cabin cruisers to take the children for rides across the lake. They also fill the camp grounds that day with farm animals the youngsters can pet and ride.

In addition to the usual camp activities, therapy is an important part of this special camp. Each youngster is given an examination by a doctor when camp begins and therapy is prescribed when it is felt necessary or that it would be beneficial. Some youngsters are sent to Woodland on the recommendation of their own doctors because of the therapy programs offered.

The largest number of those having therapy receive physical therapy. A smaller number take speech or occupational therapy, with some youngsters receiving more than one type. Therapy offices are located in a main office building and each room is well equipped with work tables, lifting bars, bicycle machines, tape recorders, or other helpful tools.

The physical therapist, speech and occupational therapists are all highly qualified workers in their fields. The physical therapy department also has a number of therapists-in-training who assist. Once the amount and type of therapy is determined, a program of activities and therapy is developed for each child.

Therapy sessions last an hour and are so scheduled that a child does not miss the same activity each time. Youngsters are pulled out of their regular activities for these sessions and are brought to and picked up from therapy by counselors. For the most part, therapy is a popular activity among the campers, and the physical therapist, especially, is one of the most respected and loved members of the camp staff.

A full-time nurse lives in camp and is available at all times. Occasionally children are taken into a nearby city for medical care provided by local hospitals and clinics.

Camp Woodland is sponsored by the State Easter Seal Society. The camp program accounts for a large part of their yearly budget and to make maximal use of this facility this year, high school students were invited to stay at the camp for periods of four days to learn more about the health fields.

In addition to handicapped children sent to camp by state agencies, campership funds were raised privately with the largest donation coming from a sizable nearby town where the local newspaper had taken up the cause. Each year they raised money to help send crippled children to Woodland. The relationship between the paper and camp personnel was a good one, and during the summer reporters came to report back to their readers what the children did at camp.

Some parents paid the entire camp fee, $50.00 a week, but according to the director, "At best, 20 percent pay a quarter of the load." The camp was eligible for government surplus food, and counselors who qualified could have their salaries paid by the college work-study program.

There was constant pressure to keep the camp filled: no small problem. All administrators in this study complained that camping has been down in recent years. Whether or not this was due to the growing use of trailers and family camping, as some camp personnel tried to explain it, the result was that the camps were concerned about attracting a maximum number of children. To meet this challenge, the director of Woodland Camp changed his policy a number of years ago and agreed to accept children with some mental retardation, as long as there was accompanying physical disorder.

According to the director, once the camp opened to the mentally retarded, there was little problem filling available space. It was also only within the last four years that Woodland has accepted severely disabled children who are in wheelchairs. When the new cabins were built and asphalt paths added, the acceptance policy could be changed. Up until that time, old log cabins were used to house the youngsters and it was necessary for campers to be able to climb stairs.

During the summer of 1970, there were ninety-six girls and boys attending Camp Woodland for the first 4-week session when the data for this study was gathered.

It was impossible to determine the amount of retardation. Medical records were often incompletely filled out by parents who tended to minimize the degree of retardation. Some children with little or no speech were difficult to assess and there was no testing of mental ability. However, through observation and interviewing of counselors and staff, an estimate is that 25 percent of the campers were mentally retarded. They ranged from a few severely retarded campers who had to be watched constantly, to slightly retarded who needed little special care and were considered educable.

Fourteen percent of all campers attending Woodland Camp were in wheelchairs, and 25 percent used braces, crutches, a prosthesis or both.* Although the entire group of campers were

---

*A few youngsters used both crutches and a wheelchair, switching back and forth depending on how fast and far they wanted to go or how tired they were. If they walked, they are not counted as being wheelchair bound here. The camp encouraged walking.

subject to our field observations, thirty-six were selected for interviews and more intensive study.

HANDICAPS

The Woodland campers had a great variety of physical disabilities (Table II). The largest group had cerebral palsy, but however similar their diagnosis, the CP children were far from similar to one another. The term, referring to brain damage, was used to describe children who had minimal motor involvement as well as others who were in wheelchairs or unable to speak. Some children with CP could participate in all activities and were only minimally slowed down; others had to be fed, toileted and

TABLE II

HANDICAPPED CHILDREN IN WOODLAND CAMP
BY DIAGNOSIS AND SEX

Diagnosis	Boys	Girls	Total
Cerebral Palsy	11	7	18
Congenital Blindness	4	2	6
Leg Perthes	1	1	2
Epilepsy	1	1	2
Cancer	1	1	2
Hydrocephaly	1	0	1
Polio	0	1	1
Albino	0	1	1
Spina Bifida	0	1	1
Muscular Dystrophy	0	1	1
Arthritis	0	1	1
Total	19	17	36

changed regularly.

While cerebral palsy was the most frequently occurring handicap, others included: impaired vision, leg perthes, epilepsy, cancer, hydrocephaly, albinism, spina bifida, muscular dystrophy and arthritis.

During the time of the study, Woodland Camp had a special program for the visually handicapped child, which accounts for the fact that nine of this group of campers had vision problems.

FUNCTIONAL ABILITY

The boys at Camp Woodland were functionally more disabled than the girls (Table III). Over half of them needed braces, crutches, had a prosthesis, or were in wheelchairs. Two boys were totally blind. There were no totally blind girls at the camp during this period and only 29 percent of the girls had hardware, crutches or were in wheelchairs. This may reflect parents' tendency to be

TABLE III

HANDICAPPED CHILDREN IN WOODLAND CAMP
BY FUNCTIONAL DISABILITY AND SEX

	Functional Disability	*Boys*	*Girls*	*Total*
Motor Coordination Affected	No Hardware	4	9*	13
	Braces, Crutches, Prostheses	5	4	9
	Wheelchairs	3	0	3
Vision Affected	Legally Blind	4	3	7
	Totally Blind	2	0	2
Speech Affected		1	1†	2
Total		19	17	36

*One child with speech affected also
†One child in wheelchair

more protective of disabled girls, thus not sending them to camp if they were severely disabled. This was the impression of Easter Seal staff involved in recruiting campers.

SOCIAL INFORMATION

Children at Camp Woodland ranged in age from six to seventeen years and tended to come from families with an average of three children. Only three campers of the thirty-six interviewed had no brothers and sisters. There were only two children whose brothers and sisters all had physical handicaps. It is safe to conclude, then, that only a few were segregated within their families from normal children. Most had normal brothers or sisters with whom they interacted in addition to friends or school mates they might have had who were not handicapped, an important fact when studying integration and segregation in terms of social participation and self concepts.

Half of the children studied went to school with normal youngsters, but this was less true for the more functionally disabled boys than the girls. Sixty-eight percent of the boys were segregated in a special school, were members of a special class within a regular school, or were taught at home by a home tutor. Only 25 percent of the girls needed special education. We must keep in mind then, that many of these children who were being studied in a segregated summer camp were not unfamiliar with integrated settings.

The boys and girls at Woodland varied also in socio-economic status. Their father's occupations ranged from professional status (doctor) to laborers (factory workers). The largest grouping (50%) was semi-skilled and manual laborers. More of the mothers worked than not (19 to 14) and these were also unskilled jobs.

Campers who attended Woodland Camp did so, in large part, for a number of years. Three fourths of the children knew others at the camp for at least two summers. The average child had been at camp three or four years.

This high repeat attendance rate, in addition to the fact that two-thirds of the counselors also were at Woodland Camp for a number of years, may account, in part, for the closeness and spirit observed among the campers and staff. The camp was predominately filled with children and counselors who had been there before and liked it enough to return.

In brief, Camp Woodland was an agency-supported camp which served children from within the state who had physical handicaps. The children were primarily from lower-middle class families. There was a great variation among campers in terms of what type disability they had and how functionally limited they were. They ranged in ages from six to seventeen, they varied in the size of their families, and whether or not they were integrated in regular school programs during the winter or segregated into special schools and classes.

Clearly, as a group, they liked Camp Woodland. Three-fourths of them were there for at least a second year and they demonstrated a liking for the camp program Woodland offered.

Chapter Four

❦❦❦❦❦❦❦❦❦❦❦❦❦❦❦❦❦❦❦❦❦❦❦❦❦❦❦❦❦❦❦❦

HIAWATHA AND CHEROKEE, INTEGRATED CAMPS

❦❦❦❦❦❦❦❦❦❦❦❦❦❦❦❦❦❦❦❦❦❦❦❦❦❦❦❦❦❦❦❦

W HEN comparing segregated and integrated camps in terms of their physical layout, one is immediately struck with the difference in terrain between the two. Both Hiawatha, a camp for girls, and Camp Cherokee for boys were geographically spread out so that campers often had a long walk over hilly, rocky ground to get between their cabins and the dining halls. Sometimes campers walked in wooded areas where the paths were strewn with roots, leaves and rocks. Both camps were located in relatively isolated wooded areas and were situated on a lake.

HIAWATHA

Hiawatha, like the other camps in this study, was an agency camp. It was sponsored by a Youth Club located in a nearby city. The camp director was also Club director during the winter months. The Club was located in the inner city and depended for membership, in large part, on children from that section of town walking into the center. Fifty percent of the campers were white, 50 percent were black.

At the beginning of each camp two-week period, children gathered at the Club and were driven to camp in a special bus. A few youngsters were brought to camp by parents or were referred to it by other social agencies, although the majority of children lived in the same area of the city and knew other campers from Club activities. Handicapped youngsters referred by the Easter Seal Society numbered from twenty to twenty-five over the entire summer, with approximately five attending each period. It was felt that it was a better policy to serve a larger number of youngsters over the whole summer for shorter camp periods than for five children to attend all summer for eight weeks.

Hiawatha's seven camper cabins housed from nine to eleven girls. One cabin had two handicapped children integrated with seven non-handicapped youngsters. Other Easter Seal children were the only handicapped members in their cabins. The cabins were built along the side of a rather steep hill. As few as possible trees had been cleared to make room for the cabins with the result being that each small, rustic building was surrounded by woods. Although other cabins actually stood nearby and were visible, the thickness of the woods gave the feeling of isolation.

Each cabin had double decker cots with a small enclosed area in one corner being the counselor's quarters. There was one counselor and one counselor-in-training in charge of each cabin. Bunkmates shared an orange crate for storing personal effects. Most clothes, however, were kept in suitcases under the beds.

There were no bathroom facilities within the cabin. Two separate buildings had large toilet rooms with multiple toilets, sinks and showers. These were located an equal distance between the athletic area and the cabin area. Near the beach there was a changing room where girls put on bathing suits for swimming.

The swimming area at the lake was divided into three pools, separated from each other by wings of the H-shaped dock. The camp owned a small number of rowboats and canoes. A cleared section of land surrounded by the cabins on one side, the beach on another, and the dining hall on the third side served as the athletic field. Here such activities as kickball, volleyball, trampoline, or tennis took place.

The camp nurse and infirmary were located on top of the hill behind the cabins and could be reached by climbing a number of steps carved into the side of the hill and formed with railroad ties. Children were examined by the camp nurse when they arrived and could go to the infirmary each morning if not feeling well. Children taking daily medication were sent each day to the nurse by their cabin counselors.

Handicapped children participated in the regular program. The camp program offered activities such as crafts, swimming, boating, trampoline, dramatics, nature and camp craft. These were supplemented with storytelling, Indian drum beating or scavenger hunts. There was a camp choir and a camp newspaper written by the children.

Cabin clean-up and camp clean-up were scheduled for each morning and all campers were expected to help. Cabins were inspected once each day and points were given according to how clean each cabin was. Awards were given at the end of each camp session to the cabin with the highest point average for the two weeks. This was the strongest evidence of scheduled competition at the camp since camp personnel tried to conduct activities for enjoyment more than competition.

Children signed up for the activities in which they wished to participate. Before breakfast, sign-up spaces were posted on the bulletin board announcing which activities were being offered that morning. There was one space for each camper provided.

For those with swimming instruction in the afternoon, two morning and one afternoon activity were available. For children with swimming instruction in the morning, two afternoon and one morning activity could be taken. Once all the blanks were filled with campers' names, an activity was closed and a child was required to sign up for another one.

Children were discouraged from repeatedly signing up for the same activities in several ways. First, a counselor could tell a child that she had been coming to such an activity as crafts too frequently and was not to sign up again for a number of days. In addition, a child's overall performance at camp was rated on how many different activities she had taken. Every youngster was given a certificate at a final campfire which rated her performance in this respect. The pressure was strong for participating in everything offered.

Children who were first to reach the sign-up board had more opportunity to choose their preferences before certain popular activities closed. Interviews with handicapped children revealed that they had had opportunities to participate in every event, although they were often forced to take an activity because all others were closed. This method of scheduling activities resulted in a mixing of children from different cabin groups. The same children never attended the same activities twice in exactly the same grouping.

All campers went to evening programs. These ranged from an evening of singing camp songs to a mid-summer Christmas party. At such events, children could play with members of other cabin groups. During the week there were a number of scheduled free periods when each youngster could take care of duties such as washing clothes, writing letters, or washing hair. Or, they could engage in informal activities with others from all over the camp.

Children attending this camp had ample opportunity for activities with members of other cabin groups, as well as free periods or all-camp programs. However, since activities were scheduled according to when a child had swimming instruction, and swimming skill is correlated with age in most cases, those of similar ages tended to be together.

Beginning instruction took place in the morning and involved mostly children nine years old or less. Older children participated in activities at this time. One fifteen year old girl with cerebral palsy was unable to pass beyond the beginning swimming level and as a result had most activities with younger children.

A large rebuilt barn housed the kitchen and dining room. It was filled with long tables flanked by benches. Counselors sat at the head and foot of the tables and did not rotate. Children, however, could pick their own table for the first few meals of the camp period. Then they were required to remain at that table for the rest of the session.

Once a week all campers could temporarily change their seat when leftovers were served and all tables were not serving the same meal. A child could pick the food and table she wished to have.

There were serving stations nearby each table, and children took turns getting the food from the counter separating the kitchen from the dining hall, and bringing it to the table. They took turns clearing the table after meals and taking dishes to the serving stations. It was felt by camp personnel that the teaching of table manners was an important aspect of this camp experience since so many children came from disadvantaged homes. Table manners were stressed by the counselors.

Sixty-five girls attended Camp Hiawatha for the two-week

period of our data collection, the first two-week session of the camping season. Five of these were girls with physical handicaps and hence the focus of intensive research.

There were two on crutches who had braces: one was 15 years old and one thirteen years old. A nine year old camper was deaf and had little speech. A fourth camper had slight CP with poor motor coordination needing daily medication. This eleven year old child was slightly retarded due to brain damage at birth. A fifth handicapped youngster, seven years old, had hydrocephaly resulting in poor motor coordination, defective vision and hearing.

CHEROKEE

Camp Cherokee, an integrated camp for boys, was sponsored by a large city YMCA. Here again, campers were selected from the YMCA membership, were referred to the camp by various city social agencies, or were sent by parents who could afford the entire camp tuition of approximately $50.00 a week. Both integrated camps received government surplus food supplies.

During the period of our study, the first two-week session, there were 123 children attending Camp Cherokee with five of these being handicapped boys referred to the camp by the Easter Seal Society. The camp accepted from five to seven handicapped youngsters each two-week session. The majority of campers attended for two weeks, with a small number staying for two sessions or a total of four weeks.

Children lived in villages, according to age groupings. Each village had from three to five cabins and served as subcamps in some respects since they were the center of activities for their members. Geographically, villages were at a distance from one another and it was only with special permission that members of different villages could visit. Some activities were arranged for two village groups. For example, a three-day overnight hike included the oldest and second oldest village groups. There were a total of five villages.

The oldest village for boys (14-16 years) had a unique arrangement. There were no cabins. The village members lived in two-man tents, camping out for the entire camp stay. They ate some meals at the main dining hall with the rest of the camp, and they cooked some of their own meals. Only one village had indoor plumbing, and the use of outhouses was a subject of much joking over the summer. Roughing it was considered a valuable part of boys' camping experience.

At Camp Cherokee, as at Hiawatha, cabin counselors served as activity leaders except for such specialties as crafts, swimming and boating. The program offered boating, swimming, field sports such as baseball, basketball and kickball. There was also tennis, archery, riflery, and nature.

Boys were asked to select their favorite activities in order of preference when they first arrived at camp. The director, head staff and village counselors then scheduled each youngster with a variety of activities according to their preference. Boys were responsible for cleaning up their cabins, the campgrounds, and being at activities when expected.

Competitive games of baseball, basketball, and other events were arranged by staff so that cabin groups competed against each other, or two villages were matched. Although enjoyment of activities was a primary goal for the camp, there was considerable emphasis on skill development, knowledge building and competition.

Free time was offered and there were arranged evening programs for the entire camp. Meals were served in a main dining room by campers who were on duty. These same campers served and cleared after meals with the on-duty position rotating to all members of a table. Boys ate at tables with cabinmates. Each day, counselors and staff selected one outstanding camper and elected him Officer-of-the-Day. With the honor of being chosen came the responsibility of being on call to the director for such tasks as showing visitors around camp or going to town with a counselor to pick up mail. There were approximately twelve boys honored with appointment to the Officer-of-the-Day position.

During the period of this study, 123 boys attended Camp Cherokee. Five were handicapped. Two had amputations: an eight year old with an arm prosthesis, and a twelve year old child with a lower leg prosthesis. A nine year old camper had a congenital heart condition and another (15 years old) had cerebral palsy due to an auto accident at seven years of age. The fifth camper (aged 15) had had polio at eighteen months and now used crutches and wore a leg brace. The two oldest campers were assigned to the same village group.

Besides the five handicapped campers, twelve non-handicapped children were studied intensively. In selecting control subjects, two non-handicapped children were selected from each cabin to which a handicapped child had been assigned. Control subjects were chosen with the help of counselors to be both representative of the normal group and as matched as possible to the handicapped child in terms of age, sex and economic status. The handicapped children and control children were interviewed and tested, were the focus of field observations and were the subject of inquiry of counselors.

SUMMARY OF CAMPS AND CAMPERS

Children attending integrated camps and those attending the segregated camp show background data of a comparable nature. Campers in both situations were of the same age range (6 to 17 years). The mean age for children at the integrated camp (10.6) was approximately one year younger than that for the segregated camp. Only 8 percent of the handicapped children at Woodland were only children, with most having two siblings. For handicapped children integrated with normal youngsters, only 5 percent were only children with one sibling being most frequent. Their normal campmates tended to come from slightly larger families with three to four siblings most common.

Socio-economic status as determined from the father's occupation also is quite similar for youngsters attending all three camps. The range in occupational status is from professional to laborer, with the predominant number being manual laborers. At Woodland Camp 26 percent of the children were from broken homes. Twenty-four percent of the integrated campers were from broken homes.

However there are some areas in which the children studied at the integrated and segregated camps differed. Handicapped children attending the integrated camps were less functionally disabled than their segregated counterparts, as could be expected. There were none in wheelchairs. It is interesting to note that although they were less handicapped, more of the campers at the integrated camp attended segregated schools or were in special classes: 60 percent compared at 48 percent in Woodland. Two non-handicapped youngsters in Camp Cherokee required special education for emotional disturbances.

As mentioned previously, the segregated camp had a high return rate among campers. Only 41 percent of the campers at Camps Hiawatha and Cherokee had been there previously compared to 75 percent of campers at Woodland who were attending for their second year or more.

There was a striking difference between the physical setup of the segregated and the two integrated camps. The physical terrain and architecture at the segregated camp was designed with the handicapped individual in mind. For handicapped children attending the regular camps, time and effort went into getting to and from buildings and activities, making beds and cleaning up or planning a visit to the infirmary.

One girl using braces and crutches was observed climbing the steep hill to the nurse's quarters on her hands and knees. After ten minutes of climbing, she reached the infirmary to learn that the nurse was no longer there. Other handicapped youngsters mentioned avoiding activities which were held in wooded areas or a far distance from the main camp because they did not want to make the effort to get there, or they felt uncomfortable about arriving after the others had begun.

Non-handicapped children and counselors expressed some concern and discomfort about having children with motor difficulties along for such activities as hiking, for they often felt obliged to stay with the slower children at the same time they felt it necessary to remain with the others who were traveling at a faster pace. Without a doubt, the physical properties and layout at the camps played an important part in the adjustment and social interaction experienced between the handicapped and non-handicapped children.

One noticeable difference between integrated and segregated camps studied was the amount of participation campers had in planning their daily activities. Children had the most opportunity to choose at the girl's integrated camp where they signed up each day for that day's activities. Choices were not only based on the activities offered, but were also influenced by who else had signed up and which counselors were going to direct the activity.

The boys at the integrated camp had a choice in which activities they were to be assigned. However, once programs were scheduled, the groups were set. Children had the same activities throughout the camp session and these were always led by the same counselors.

Campers had no choice in program selections at Woodland Camp. All children attended all activities offered. Groups of cabin members were taken to the various activities by their cabin counselors who helped with each activity directed by a special staff counselor. It was the counselors who had the responsibility for knowing what activities were in a day's schedule and seeing that the campers got to them on time.

In terms of having responsibility for themselves, there was a difference between programming at the two types of camps. Children integrated had more responsibility in terms of being places on time and getting around the camp grounds.

While this difference could be attributed to the specific camps studied for this project, it is felt that the tighter control over the handicapped children at the segregated camp was, in part, a result of the camp staff and counselor philosophy in dealing with handicapped children. This will be discussed further in the next chapter.

Chapter Five

COUNSELORS AND THE
COMMITMENT TO SEGREGATION

MANY people came into contact with campers, but the cabin counselors were closest with them during their stay. Counselors lived in the cabins with the children, had activities with them and were directly responsible for their care, helping with personal difficulties and seeing that they had fun.

THOSE WHO CHOSE TO WORK
WITH HANDICAPPED CHILDREN

Everyone working at Woodland Camp talked about the strong group spirit among counselors the year of this study. The director, staff and counselors themselves often mentioned their group *esprit de corps,* adding at times that this was the best group of counselors ever. Field observations described an ease and comfort among the group, seeking each other out to talk during free periods, a willingness to help each other, as well as pairing off between some boy and girl counselors.

There was a relatively low amount of clique formation observed at the segregated camp as compared to the integrated camps. There was some conflict between cabin counselors and the program staff, however. The former resented the fact that the program staff had only three periods of work for the entire day, yet according to the counselors, still depended upon cabin counselors for activity ideas and keeping the activities running well.

Some program staff, on the other hand, resented the counselors for looking down on them and for thinking that the staff did not work as hard as they felt they did. However, the closeness between counselors existed and was attributed by them to several facts.

There was a high return rate. Sixty-three percent had been together during the past two to five summers; four out of five were college students, with a large percentage attending one or another branch of the State University. Many counselors retained friendships over winter months while at school. In addition, counselors shared an interest in working with handicapped children and often talked about the sense of purpose they all had.

Of thirty-one cabin counselors at the camp, we interviewed twenty-four, four from each cabin. Also interviewed were six program counselors.

When asked what their future goals were, answers ranged from vague replies such as, "I want to do something with the physical disabled child," usually given by individuals just entering college, to more specific answers from counselors who were more advanced in their schooling and had already taken prerequisites or special training courses for such fields as physical or speech therapy. Obviously, working with handicapped children attracted these counselors and it is not surprising that two-thirds of them planned careers in this area. But why were they attracted to this field?

One answer to this question might be that many of them knew a handicapped person previously. Three-quarters of the counselors said that they had known someone with a disability. Four mentioned relatives. Others said that they had a handicapped neighbor, knew a youngster in school or had volunteered to work with handicapped, retarded or emotionally disturbed people.

Counselors were asked if they themselves had a handicap, and there seems to be an important difference between men and women in the way they answered. Two-thirds of the male counselors said they had some handicaps, mentioning the following disorders: asthma, severe allergies, epilepsy, cerebral palsy, and legal blindness without glasses. Three of the male counselors answered that they had such handicaps as, "not living up to my potential in school," or "I have to prove myself all the time," and "I mumble when I meet new people and can't be heard." Only one female counselor counted her short temper as a handicap and none mentioned a medical disorder of any sort.

This striking difference between the males and females attracted to working with handicapped children may be due to the fact that females in our sample are more representative of females in general, while the male counselors are not typical of men in general, many of whom might not be attracted to working with disabilities. Such helping roles are usually considered female roles and as such probably attract women more readily than men.

What brings men to work with disabled children? Almost all of them said that they had known people with handicaps whereas only half the women counselors said they did. It is possible that knowing a handicapped individual personally or feeling that one has a handicap oneself leads to wanting to participate in such an occupation.

Would counselors at Woodland Camp accept jobs at a regular camp for normal children? Two-thirds of both men and women said that they would not. They felt that they would not want to work with normal children if they could be with handicapped youngsters. Thus, the counselors at Camp Woodland were select in terms of liking the camp, liking to work with handicapped children specifically and of fitting into the camp system so that they were asked back for the job. The camp director had a large number of applications despite the demanding work and strict hiring policy.

In commenting on the counselor staff, the director said:

> I think it's a hell of a lot more work here than it would be at another camp. No doubt about it for the counselors: they work themselves to the bone. On their days off, some counselors go check into a motel room and just sleep the whole time.

> Our pay scale is much lower than it would be at a private camp too. Yet the work is so rewarding, I wouldn't have it any other way and neither would some of the counselors.

From interview 7/9/70

Since the children needed special attention, there was a 1:3 ratio of counselors to campers at Camp Woodland. Each cabin group of approximately sixteen youngsters had five counselors. In comparison, at the regular camps there were one counselor and one counselor-in-training for cabins of twelve children, a ratio of 1:6. As mentioned in the previous chapter, children were assigned to cabins at Woodland according to their age, primarily. However they were selected so that no group of counselors was overloaded with children who needed a great deal of attention. There were usually two children in wheelchairs and four with braces or crutches in each cabin of sixteen campers.

ATTITUDES TOWARD WORK

It was a rule of the camp that all children be accompanied by a counselor at all times. And it was the same counselors who slept in the cabins with the children who remained with their group for the entire day's activities save for swimming and special events. The cabin counselors attended games and activities with these same children, ate with them and were responsible for their safety and physical and emotional needs.

A job description can differ greatly from what an individual actually does or how he describes his work. It is also possible for individual counselors to feel differently about what their job entails although they are theoretically holding the same position. We asked cabin counselors directly to describe their work. Physical care of the children was the most frequently mentioned task.

Counselors also said that they were working to see that the kids had fun or made good psychological adjustments. Table IV indicates the range of responses to the question, "How Would You Describe Your Job?"

Physical care of these children sometimes reached a degree of intimacy not experienced between adults and children after the latter pass infancy. The counselors helped some children use the toilet; they dressed and undressed youngsters from age six to sixteen years. They put on braces, gave out medications, and at times set alarms so they could awaken during the night to help someone turn over in bed or go to the toilet.

It is not surprising that a closeness developed between cabin counselors and campers. In general, this closeness was not duplicated in the integrated situations, except possibly between

TABLE IV

COUNSELORS' RESPONSES TO THE QUESTION: "HOW WOULD YOU DESCRIBE YOUR JOB?"

Response	*No.*	*Percent*
A. Physical Care (Picking them up, braces, feeding, clothing, cleaning, toileting, diaper changing).	15	50

"I take care of the kids, taking care of their braces, um, making sure the braces are always right, are on right, taken off right, see that they're fed, their clothes are clean, um see nothing is wrong. Like with Jimmy, yesterday, his braces made him red from rubbing so I had to give him a rub down and that stuff. . . ."

"My job is just living with the kids all day, getting up in the morning, you know, physically dressing kids, helping them feed themselves and talking to them and laughing with them. . . ."

"I go around to activities with them and spend most of the day pulling clothes on and taking clothes off. Taking kids to the john at night is the worse thing I have to do. . . ."

B. See That Kids Have Fun	5	17

"My job is to help the kids have a good time while they're here. . . ."

". . . to let them enjoy themselves. They get little enough fun at home."

C. Teach Skills	4	13

". . . it's teaching them, helping them, talking to them, trying to make them as independent as you can, by not doing things for them. If they want you to dress them, you make them dress themselves."

"I want to teach them how to get along with people."

"To help the kids see what life is really like; that there are rules in life that they have to live by. Like you can't have your way all the time."

D. Helping with Psychological Adjustment	3	10

"My job is helping them understand their problems."

"I try to help them adjust to their handicaps. That's my goal."

Response	*No.*	*Percent*
E. Discipline Them	3	10

"I have to get them to obey and do things they are supposed to do."

"My job is getting easier now since they have learned what we counselors expect of them."

one or two counselors and a small number of children.

At the special camp, the closeness at times turned into a protectiveness towards the children. Witness the protectiveness expressed by a counselor while discussing the possibility of having meetings with other camp personnel. The meetings were proposed for counselors and staff to discuss problems they encountered in their work. Such an idea was being attacked by a male counselor:

I certainly wouldn't want, and I don't think anyone else would want, say someone in Cabin One — discussing my kids because they don't know what goes on in my cabin and I wouldn't be able to discuss their kids.

From tape-recorded group
meeting 7/17/70

COUNSELORS' ATTITUDES TOWARD
HANDICAPPED CHILDREN

In addition to mentioning closeness to campers that was often accompanied by physical intimacy, three-quarters of the counselors interviewed said that the handicapped were different from normal children — better than normal youngsters.

Counselors had not been asked directly whether they considered handicapped children to be different from non-handicapped ones. However, several interview questions were designed to see if there was an attitude toward handicapped children shared by those who worked with them so closely. For example, when asked if they would take a job at a regular camp, counselors were probed for why they felt the way they did.

Most expressed some feelings that handicapped children were special. Six of those who mentioned a difference said that normal children were more spoiled: "I couldn't work with normal children who are always complaining about nothing. They're spoiled rotten and they don't know it."

Six said that handicapped children are more needy, need more love. And ten of those expressing a positive attitude toward physically handicapped children attributed better personality traits to them. Several commented that handicapped children were more appreciative:

> . . . like with these kids, you give them a little and as far as they're concerned, it's the entire world. They're so happy no matter what you give them, but with normal kids, you give them a little and they will ask for more.

From interview 7/7/70

Others mentioned that handicapped children show more love and affection; are more beautiful inside; cheerful and happy. Only six of the counselors interviewed made no mention of handicapped children being different from normal youngsters, although some of these preferred to work with the handicapped.* Perhaps such a bias towards those one serves increases ones positive attitude toward the actual work, which at times was unpleasant and physically demanding for the counselors.

It is evident thus far, that this group of workers felt close to the children and, in fact, saw handicapped children as superior to normal youngsters. This positive attitude towards those they served was augmented by a positive attitude toward the special camp. When asked about the purpose of a segregated camp like Camp Woodland, 60 percent of the counselors thought segregation provided children who had physical handicaps with opportunities they would not get elsewhere. It was by segregating them that they could be relieved of being made to feel different. Table V shows the range in attitudes of counselors when they were directly asked what they felt the purpose of a segregated camp was.

Treating handicapped children normally has high priority and

---

*There have been a number of studies which show extreme attitudes toward the physically handicapped individual. See: Mussen, P. H. and Barker, R. G., "Attitudes Toward Cripples," *Journal of Abnormal and Social Psychology,* 39, 1944, 351-355, which shows how some college students rated cripples favorably on all scales while others tended to generalize negatively about them.

TABLE V

COUNSELORS' RESPONSES TO THE QUESTION:
"WHAT DO YOU SEE AS THE PURPOSE OF A CAMP LIKE THIS?"

Response	*No.*	*Percent*
A. Give the Children Opportunities They Wouldn't Get Elsewhere: Remove Children from Being Handicapped or Different the Rest of the Year	18	60

"Like camp makes it as normal an experience for them as possible. You can't say it's entirely normal. Everything has to be geared to them, but I think you don't have to let them know. For them it's a normal experience."

"To help handicapped children enjoy themselves at least for a little while where in other circumstances they probably wouldn't be able to enjoy themselves."

"Normally they can't compete. They're beaten down time and time again. Here they compete with kids who are more or less handicapped and they can do well and it gives them a chance to see that they aren't worthless."

"Most of these kids are disregarded by other kids; they're seen as strange: something one should keep away from. But here, I mean, they're all the same, you know, and everyone has a problem and everyone knows everyone here has a problem and it's great. A great place for the kids."

"We're just one place in their lives where we're trying to treat them as completely normal. Like you've seen us saying 'hurry up' and things like that. We don't treat them differently at all."

B. Get the Kids Away from Their Parents	6	20

"The purpose is to get the kids away from parents who don't care. Some parents just dump them here to get rid of them."

"To get them away from being babied and spoiled."

"I can just see them watching TV all day and it's really sad. Here they are active and can do all sorts of things."

Responses	*No.*	*Percent*
C. Help Them to Develop	3	10

"There are a lot of emotional hang-ups that go with being handicapped and parents are too close and have their own hang-ups to help. Hopefully an attentive counselor can help the child adjust to his handicap and get a realistic perception of himself."

"It gets them away from self-sorrow because it gives them a chance to see that no matter how bad off you are, there's always someone who's worse off."

D. Provide Therapies	3	10

since the physically handicapped children are not felt to be completely normal, the belief expressed here is that placed in a special environment, they can be treated as normal and thus feel normal. This perspective leads to a belief which we call *Commitment to Segregation;* the way to make the physically handicapped child *feel normal* is to arrange a special environment in which he can *do normal things;* play baseball, have craft projects, swim, and so forth. Such a child must be removed from competition, play and other activities with non-handicapped youngsters so that he can compete more fairly.

When asked specifically, only one-quarter of the counselors stated that they thought integrating one or two handicapped children into a cabin with non-handicapped youngsters was a good idea. The rest had reservations about it or felt that it could not possibly work out. They said such things as:

Normal children wouldn't accept the handicapped kids and they get enough of that the rest of the year.

It would be unfair competition and the handicapped child would lose out all the time.

Maybe if the handicaps were really minor so that they'd have an equal chance, but the normal kids would have to be hand-picked and the handicapped kids would have to be, too — it's too complicated and probably wouldn't work.

From interviews
7/6/70 — 7/9/70

COMMITMENT TO SEGREGATION

Emphasis was upon changing the social setting so that physically handicapped children could feel normal. This perspective is based on several assumptions shared by counselors at the integrated camps, and most Americans as well.*

One assumption is that there is a normal way of life; a normal childhood or normal group experiences which lead to having a normal youth.

> Here they can play baseball, make things in crafts, go boating and swimming. When I tell outsiders about my job, I stress the normal things we do so that they will know we're a camp just like any other camp.

From interview 7/7/70

There are similarities in the programs offered at most camps whether for normal or handicapped children. Certain sports and activities are assumed to be wholesome, good experiences, necessary for the developing boy or girl, normal or handicapped. All American girls should make projects in crafts and all children should boat and swim and learn how to build campfires with wood collected in the woods. Such experiences are seen as leading to positive social and emotional development.

The Easter Seal *Guide to Special Camping Programs* (1968) states:

> The philosophy of organizations interested in the area of special camp programs may be allied to the following general concepts:
>
> 1. Persons with special needs should be afforded the same rewarding experiences that are available to the non-handicapped. . . .
>
> 3. The social-recreational values to be derived from association with nature through camping are inherently therapeutic without regard to any concomitant medical or paramedical benefits that may

---

*The perspective *Commitment to Integration* at the integrated camps placed the emphasis on changing the handicapped person's performance, not the setting. The individual was helped to meet normal standards of the given setting. This *commitment to integration* was based upon the same basic assumptions as *commitment to segregation* and will be discussed in the next chapter.

accrue.... (p. 2).

The Guide continues:

> The camp should be as nearly similar to a camp for the non-handicapped as it is possible to make it, deviating only when necessary. (p. 4).

The first assumption is that there is a normal program for youth, and a second assumption is that everyone has a right to be normal. There appears to be a basic American value that everyone should be like others, not different, not deviant. Goffman talks about how those with a stigma are expected to act as if normal and to remove themselves when their difference would be too apparent for the non-handicapped to overlook:

> The nature of a "good adjustment" is now apparent. It requires that the stigmatized individual cheerfully and unselfconsciously accept himself as essentially the same as normals, while at the same time he voluntarily withholds himself from those situations in which normals would find it difficult to give lip service to their similar acceptance of him. (Goffman, 1963, p. 121)

Beatrice Wright discusses this idea and shows how the concept of the physically handicapped person as deviant implies this accepted normal standard:

> It might be suggested that the concept of physical disability implies deviation from a normal standard, deviation from a state that is natural or average.... (Wright, 1960, p. 8)

The right to be normal, or the push to be normal, is a value which, however, leads to conflicts with reality for there are those individuals who do not have equal ability or average appearance, or do not have the interest or social opportunities to be normal. An example is the child who possesses musical genius and prefers playing a piano to playing baseball; he is often of concern to parents who worry about his growing up normally.

Many equal opportunities programs have sprung into existence to provide the culturally disadvantaged child with opportunities to develop and experience normal and worthwhile activities enjoyed by the white middle class child.

The philosophical approach, commitment to segregation, implies that the way to make a physically handicapped child feel normal is to arrange a special environment in which he can do normal things. To feel normal, the assumption is that one must be doing the expected, normal activities. The special environment entails removing the child from competition, play and other activities with non-handicapped youngsters so he can compete more fairly. By excluding normal children from the special camps, the handicapped child is no longer different from those playing with him, no longer a permanent loser, and thus able for perhaps the first time in his life to partake in such normal experiences. These values are shared by campers as well as counselors and staff.

According to Woodland campers as well as the entire staff, an annually held evening program called "Night Club" is the highlight of the entire camping season. The camp's dining hall is decorated as a night club and the children arrive with their dates for an experience that "they have never had before and may never experience again." The director describes the evening as follows:

> This is the big event; this is the thing the kids think about from the opening day.

> It's something to see — to see the kids in the dining hall decorated like a night club. The counselors put on "Cabaret" for them or a floor show or something of this nature and here are the kids trying to act so grown-up with their pizzas and their little pink "champagne", and they're all dressed in suits and ties and they've gotten a "corsage" for their girls. You know, they have to go pick them up and it's a chance to kiss a girl goodnight, too, which is something that many of them haven't done.

> And you know, they're talking about it weeks ahead of time and it's funny; it's touching. I think it's of lasting value. It gives them a chance to think, well, I'm not really that different.

> From interview with
> director 7/14/70

Commitment to Segregation is based on the assumptions implied in the above description of the Night Club evening. Such experiences as having a date which requires a corsage, a good-night kiss, and so forth, are the makings of a non-deviant life. However, it is through segregating the handicapped children (removing non-handicapped children) that the child with a physical disability can participate in such valued activities which, it is assumed, will result in his feeling normal.

The segregated camp, therefore, can be seen as a means to allow a functionally limited child to be normal by doing the normal things, though not in the normal way or the way of the majority. This is accomplished in the main by new definitions of ways to do things, which will be discussed in the chapter on Programming.

It will suffice in focusing on counselors' commitment to segregation to consider their role in promoting the success of this philosophy. The new rules which ensure a feeling of normalcy on the part of participants can only be successful if the usual rules, the rules of the majority are not available for comparison.

Normal children are, of course, not enrolled in the special camp. Counselors and staff expressed distrust of outsiders who visited, often complaining to the director that they felt "watched", uncomfortable and that they were being judged by people who "didn't understand." To understand required becoming so immersed in the system that other values and standards no longer serve as a measure for behavior. The following excerpt from fieldnotes shows how one's perspective can change when in a segregated situation.

Patty [counselor] told me how Christina [counselor] had done "her thing" yesterday and how everyone was still laughing about it. Christina's thing — which she has done for a number of years — is to sit in one of the wheelchairs and "cripple" herself up when visitors are coming through. According to Patty, Christina starts drooling, moves her head back and forth in spastic motions and grunts — uh, uh, uh.

Apparently one of the women visiting yesterday stopped at her chair to say hello and Christina, supposedly excited by the visit, started grunting louder while moving about wildly. The woman didn't know what to do and just hurried away. The kids, luckily, held their laughter back until she was gone.

While telling me about the incident, Patty was laughing hard. I also found the whole thing extremely funny. I laugh as I write these notes — but why? I know I'll never get anyone else who isn't here to laugh about it, and perhaps when away from here I won't laugh either.

From fieldnotes 7/13/70

Commitment to Segregation, thus, creates a homogeneous grouping which then establishes its own norms and therefore a feeling of normalcy for participants who do not feel normal away from the special setting. The counselors are not explicitly given this philosophy but it is clearly their commonly shared role to defend the system and promote belief in it.

Chapter Six

><><><><><><><><><><><><><><><><><><><><><><><><><><

COUNSELORS AND THE
COMMITMENT TO INTEGRATION

><><><><><><><><><><><><><><><><><><><><><><><><><><

Lıke their counterparts at the segregated camp, most counselors at the integrated camps were college students. However the interests and occupational goals of this group were not as homogeneous. Future goals of the integrated counselors ranged from housewife to entering the ministry.

Most male counselors were preparing for professional careers such as ornithology, marine biology, history or pediatrics. Their reasons for coming to camp as counselors varied, with some saying that they would have preferred other work but were unable to find another job. Several male counselors who participated in college sports said that they chose to work at a camp because it kept them in good physical shape.

The girls' and boys' camps each had a counselors' cabin, a place where staff could congregate when off-duty, exchange stories, talk, read and rest away from campers. Having such a retreat added to the positive relationships among counselors although the closeness and *esprit de corps* did not approximate that found among those working with the handicapped children at the special camp.

Out of the eighteen cabin counselors at the boys' camp, eight were interviewed. Of the ten cabin counselors at the girls' camp, five were interviewed. They were chosen to represent cabins to which handicapped children had been assigned and the activities in which they participated. In addition four male and two female program counselors were interviewed.

The ratio of counselors to campers was lower at the integrated camps. Obviously less care was needed for normal children. During the period of the research, the boys' and girls' camps had ratios of counselors to children of 1:6. Counselors in the integrated camps did not spend most of the day with the same group of youngsters. They were responsible for a cabin group and doubled as activities leaders except for special activities such as waterfront and crafts. In the course of a day a counselor came into contact with a large number of campers other than those in his or her cabin.

In comparing the staff of the camps studied, what seemed to be missing most among the integrated counselors was the sense of purpose, or shared interest in helping campers, which was found among those working at Woodland Camp.

Not only were the majority of the latter attracted to camping with the handicapped child, they were attracted enough to the entire field to plan on making it their future work. At the non-special camps, most female counselors were anticipating vocations involving children, but only one of the male counselors indicated this goal (pediatrician), and only two female counselors mentioned working with the handicapped or emotionally disturbed child.

COUNSELORS' ATTITUDES TOWARD HANDICAPPED CHILDREN

A major difference between counselors at the integrated and segregated camps was that those at Woodland Camp *chose* to work with handicapped children while those at the integrated camp had taken jobs as counselors in a regular camp yet had had handicapped children assigned to their cabin *regardless of their feelings.* A few counselors expressed dislike of working with the handicapped children while others were positive about the experiences they had had.

> *Male Counselor:* I say to myself, I don't want anything to do with them [handicapped campers] because I don't have any patience. I just can't. . . . And besides, doing too much for kids is not good anyway.
>
> From interview 7/19/69

> *Female Counselor:* I'd like to work with handicapped children some

day. Frankly, I would like a cabin of all handicapped girls. They would listen to me more than the normal girls who are wise-guys.

From interview 7/8/69

During interviews and often in informal conversations, counselors at the integrated camps discussed problems they felt they had encountered because handicapped children had been integrated into their cabin groups. Would they have liked special training? Only three said that they would have appreciated a booklet or movie telling them specifically what to expect from the handicapped campers. Ten said that they would not benefit from training if there could have been any anyway. They preferred to:

Take things as they go. That's what I always say. The kids we have are doing fine. They all mix perfectly.

It doesn't help much to discuss the kids. I don't see how there could be any special training. Each child is an individual; different in their needs and capabilities.

You don't need training; you've just got to accept them as a person, an individual.

From interviews
7/6/69 to 7/9/69

"You've just got to accept them as a person, an individual." Perhaps one of the reasons counselors at the integrated camps felt training was unnecessary was that it would negate the individuality of each handicapped child. They tended to distrust any process which grouped the handicapped children together or generalized about them.

The Easter Seal Society which assigned children to camp also provided an orientation for camp directors and counselors. They followed up on children's adjustment to camp, and were available for consultation throughout the summer. At times they removed a child from a camp if adjustment seemed too difficult.

The orientation program for counselors during the week before the campers arrived usually consisted of a lecture by Easter Seal Society representatives. The talk described handicapped children in general, their social and emotional needs, their physical and medical needs and possible difficulties they might have in playing with non-handicapped children. Counselors were also told about the twenty or so specific children who would be attending their camp during one of the four two-week periods of the summer.

Counselors were asked about this orientation when interviewed. They found it to be of little or no help. They stated that specific information about the handicapped children placed in their cabin groups would have been helpful and welcomed if given *after* they knew the individual children.

Each child was seen as an individual and information about them was thought only valuable when counselors actually knew them and understood some of their problems. The rejection of general information about children with handicaps fits with the philosophical approach shared by counselors at the camps and discussed during orientation week. As several counselors summed it up:

Stress is on the individual. In pre-camp we talk about philosophy of the camp, and so forth. We talk about our basic approach to kids as human beings and so forth. Basically people get indoctrinated before the kids really come. . . .

The basic philosophy of loving and accepting every child as a human being who has needs and desires, but they're all different. And to treat them as human beings, and to deal with them as human beings, and, ah, to live with them for two weeks or a month. And let them have as much fun while they're here. That's what I believe.

That question would get back to my whole philosophy of how you approach any child who is handicapped. It's the way we approach all our children, you know. They're just all on a par, and we expect the same things of everyone, and if they need special help, anybody, we'll try and give it to them.

From interviews with
female counselors
7/6/69 to 7/9/69

COMMITMENT TO INTEGRATION

As the last statement quoted above suggests, everyone is seen as an individual, all equally sharing rights and responsibilities. There is an implied commitment to integrating handicapped campers with the non-handicapped youngsters shared by counselors and staff working at the boys' and girls' camps.

The handicapped, as all children, are seen as individuals with the right to participate in normal activities. When help was seen as being needed to enable them to perform with the others and fit into group activities, they would be given help. The help was to compensate for the handicapped child's functional disability when performing camp activities. There was no categorical group, such as handicapped children, acknowledged by the counselors. These children were seen as individuals who needed help at times when playing group activities.

In like manner, black and white children (the girls' camp was approximately 50 percent white, 50 percent black) were seen as exactly alike, individuals with individual differences. As the staff saw it, there was no reason for blacks grouping together, as there was no reason for handicapped children grouping together.

The successful integration of the physically handicapped child seemed to hinge on an open denial of their disabilities, difference or deviancy. Among those committed to integration of the deviant, there were subtle forces preventing segregation no matter how part-time.

The director at Hiawatha said that she made table arrangements and other groupings of youngsters to prevent Negro children from grouping together.* No overt mention was made of preventing handicapped children from seeking each other out, but it did seem that such grouping was somehow suspect to the staff.

The fact is that handicapped children did not seek each other as companions often. And, as if aware of the forces to keep them from banding together, handicapped youngsters would often communicate with each other if seemingly alone or unnoticed. For example, a young girl with crutches was

---

*There was no injunction against white girls making sub-groupings although the racial mix was equal in the camp. This clearly demonstrates an attempt to deny a *deviant* condition, with black considered deviant in this group because it is so considered in the larger society.

observed indicating to another youngster using crutches where easy paths lay by simply pointing. No words were exchanged, yet they seemed to know each other's problems. Some embarrassment was expressed by the older girl when she realized one of the researchers had observed this exchange.

The Commitment to Integration is a perspective shared by the camp personnel, non-handicapped and handicapped campers in this setting. It involved a belief that for the best results, physical disabilities should not be openly acknowledged.

By those working at the integrated camps, it was considered a kindness to keep normal children from asking handicapped youngsters questions about their disabilities. The following describes an incident where counselors stopped a normal child from examining an arm prosthesis, although the handicapped boy did not seem to mind the exchange.

> *Male counselor:* During the first few days of camp I was very apprehensive about how the kids would adjust to David's arm. Thank God, the kids were great, but we had one problem.
>
> A fellow from another village came down to our table one evening. He was the only kid who I heard actually confront him with a series of questions; bullet-like questions as to "how does the arm work?"
>
> David was trying to eat dinner and the kid grabbed him, his mechanical arm, and was looking at it and trying to. . . . He started right at the wrist and asked him right up to the shoulder, pulled his sleeve and wanted to know. . . . David cooperated with it all. It didn't bother him one single bit but I put a stop to it.

From interview 7/18/69

Another counselor recalled the following incident:

> *Male Counselor:* Some real wise-guy started trouble one day. Steve took off his, ah, other leg [lower leg prosthesis] and laid it down beside his bed. This nut started asking him about it, but that didn't last long because we straightened that situation out.
>
> *Interviewer:* What did you do?
>
> *Counselor:* I gave it to the kid. You know, I said if he didn't care

about other people's feelings you know, I'd. . . . But he's a wise-guy anyway. Nobody said anything.

From interview 7/17/69

There were many illustrative stories told by counselors of non-handicapped children talking *about* the handicapped children but not directly to them. As one counselor stated:

Counselor: I'm pleased it's a mature enough group so that they're not going to hurt him . . . to make fun of him to his face. They'll laugh at him behind his back but not to his face. . . .

From interview 7/18/69

The counselors felt that handicapped children had the right to such a camping experience and that they should be treated as normal. No mention was openly made about having physical handicaps. In fact, any attempt to group children by nature of having handicaps was reacted to negatively. When asked, 75 percent of the counselors said that unless handicapped children were really disabled, they should not be segregated. Segregation was seen as emphasizing the fact of the disability which would result in getting further from normal lives than integrating the children was assumed to do.

As was to be expected, the handicapped child often presented a problem to the counselors when he or she was expected to perform with the normal children. In some cases they could not do so at all. In other cases their performance was slower or substantially below that of the non-physically disabled children so that the counselors were faced with the difficulty of leading activities where abilities varied significantly.

The philosophical approach used by the counselors was to see each child as an individual and to supplement poor performance with help when necessary so that such a person could be integrated into the regular camp activities. In this way, the handicapped child would be brought as close to normal as possible. This was the perspective, *commitment to integration.*

COMPARING PHILOSOPHIES

There were some basic assumptions and values shared by all

counselors in this study regardless of which camp employed them.

Value One: All individuals have the right (obligation) to be as normal as possible. The physically handicapped child should be made to feel normal.

Value Two: Certain activities in our culture are valued for their assumed ability to enhance children's development. Camping activities: sports, crafts, swimming, and so forth, provide normal childhood experiences important for children's development.

Where the two types of camps differed greatly was in their approach to providing these normal experiences. Since the physically handicapped child was not physically normal, the segregated camps provided sports and other activities which were adapted for the physically disabled. They compensated for deficiencies by excluding comparison with normal children thus providing them with experiences which would make them feel normal.

In other words, activities were altered so that the handicapped child could play and feel normal and have normal experiences denied him when non-handicapped children were present. Physical differentness was not overlooked but recognized and dealt with directly in therapies and in arranging the activities.

The philosophical approach shared by counselors working at the integrated camps was that treating the handicapped children as normal provided the best opportunities for them to feel normal. This required an overlooking of physical disabilities, a silencing of open acknowledgment of disabilities, and an effort to help handicapped children fit into regular camp activities. The individual was helped in this performance so that he could be a regular member of the group activities. They had a commitment to integration of the physically handicapped youngster. Their counterparts at Woodland Camp had a commitment to segregation.

Although seemingly opposite philosophies, the two approaches are similar in that they each attempt to create a homogeneous grouping within which normalcy is defined and can be achieved by all participants. In each case the sense of homogeneity is maintained by defenses against recognition of subgroups whose standards may differ from those of the main group.

Chapter Seven

><><><><><><><><><><><><><><><><><><><><><><><><><><><><><><><><><><

PROGRAMMING IN
THE SEGREGATED CAMP

><><><><><><><><><><><><><><><><><><><><><><><><><><><><><><><><><><

ONE goal of Camp Woodland was to provide the handicapped child with a normal experience and the camp program was designed so that a child's physical limitations would not hinder participation in activities.*

The segregated camp program offered boating and swimming, crafts, field sports, dramatics, and nature, as well as camp crafts and overnight trips for each cabin group. No matter how severely handicapped, a child was expected to participate in all activities. The following excerpt from fieldnotes describes cabin clean-up and how a severely disabled child was brought into the activity despite her low functional ability.

> I watched cabin clean-up in Cabin Two today. Everyone was busy somewhere. Alice [crutches, poor motor coordination] laboriously spent the entire time (45 minutes) making her bed while mumbling humorously that she didn't want her mother to know she could make her bed herself.
>
> Cathy [autistic] was being led around by Patty [counselor] to see what still needed to be done. The more able children were helping others make beds, sweep and clean the bathrooms.
>
> Christina [counselor] asked Beryl [wheelchair, involved arms] what she had been assigned today. When Beryl said she was supposed to empty the trash basket, Christina with mock anger said, "Well, let's get moving." Christina picked up the waste paper can and placed it on Beryl's lap. Keeping her hands on it to steady it, the counselor pushed Beryl out to the main garbage cans. Christina emptied the basket and

---

*Providing therapy was another main goal of the segregated camp. Therapy is not a main concern of the present study and will be brought in only to the extent that it influenced programming and camp life.

then replaced it on Beryl's lap. She wheeled her back to the cabin announcing that Beryl had done her job.

From fieldnotes 6/20/70

In the above incident, it would have been easier for the counselor to empty the trash herself than to push Beryl along with her. However, cabin members performed tasks and activities together and as a group; every child was expected to participate. On the other hand, as everyone readily admitted, the abilities of the children in cabin groups and in the camp as a whole differed significantly.

Counselors were asked specifically how the children in their cabins functioned as a group. In only two cases did counselors claim their cabins made a good grouping. Most had reservations. However, whether or not they thought the grouping was good, counselors categorized the important differences between children in terms of physical and mental functioning, and maturity of children's interest. Table VI shows how counselors conceived the differences between children.

Woodland Camp was organized so that everyone was expected to participate, yet individuals differed greatly, not only in terms of their physical functioning but also in terms of their mental abilities and interests. Some campers were not able to talk or move other than with spastic movements. They were usually in wheelchairs.

A number of the more physically disabled children were considered among the most intelligent of the campers despite lack of speech. Still other campers at Woodland had virtually no physical disabilities but were so retarded they needed constant supervision to see that they did not wander off or hurt themselves. Physically, they could play ball, if they could be taught to understand the rules.

Given the expectation that all children were to participate in the camp's program and the variety of abilities, the question had to be faced: How could activities be arranged so that everyone could participate?

Attempts to resolve this conflict involved either (1) grouping children to minimize differences, or (2) changing games to

TABLE VI

CABIN COUNSELORS' IN CAMP WOODLAND RESPONSES TO THE QUESTION:
"DO THE CHILDREN IN YOUR CABIN MAKE A GOOD GROUPING? WHY?"

Responses	*No.*	*Percent*
Yes	2	8

"This is the best group I've ever had. In the past there have been cliques. But this year, all around I've got six counselors and 16 kids and we get along perfectly."

"They make a real good grouping because I don't have any real vegetables that just lay there and can't do anything. They can all do most things."

No, Not Entirely	22	92

1. Difference in Physical Abilities (12)

"I don't think in a camp like this you'll ever have a good grouping. We've got severely handicapped and we've got almost no handicaps, and in between. As a cabin itself, it's not one group, no. They get along well, but in activities they are really different."

"Well, my cabin's sort of split really. I've got six or seven that are really active and about two or three that just sit around reading or playing cards. They form cliques. Then you've got the wheelchairs that can't run around at all."

"Some of the kids just can't participate in any way in many of the activities we have. It works the other way, too. There are activities we don't have which we should for some of the more capable children."

2. Difference in Mental Abilities (16)

"The critical thing is intelligence. Like Richard [retarded, involved speech]. He has a handicap which is irritating in the group situation. He'll talk nonsense and scream at bedtime. Now if Richard were a wheelchair case and could reason fairly normally, such a problem would disappear."

"There are really different levels of functioning. You know, how do you work so everyone is happy? You could amuse Sammy with something that Burt Caseman would rather die than do."

"We have a split in our cabin as far as mentality goes. Some kids are at the age where they know what they're doing; their personalities are developed, while others are just kids, not interested in the same things at all."

compensate for deficiencies. At various times during the camp season, children were *grouped by functional ability.* At other times, children were engaged in *parallel play.* While participating together in the same activity, some youngsters performed the more demanding tasks while others did the simpler ones, which were usually more peripheral to the game. Thus children were placed in *core roles and para roles.*

GROUPING BY FUNCTIONAL ABILITY

Given the mixed group of participants, grouping children by functional ability is one way to ensure everyone will have a chance to play. Although this type of programming was not frequent, there were two special events scheduled where handicapped children at Camp Woodland were grouped by functional abilities. During the period of this research, there were two Olympic Event Days: Sports Day and Water Olympics.

Sports Day consisted of relay races and other field events. Children were assigned to teams and activities by counselors and staff who decided beforehand who could compete against whom fairly. For example, a relay race was run between teams of children having little or no motor difficulty: those who were perhaps legally blind, epileptic or albino.

To make the chances equal for each team, an older boy with cerebral palsy who had slight motor involvement in one leg was matched against a girl several years his junior who had no motor involvement. Children in wheelchairs were matched against each other and each was assigned a counselor who would run toward the finish line pushing the chairs as fast as possible.

Towards the end of the first session, the water meet was held. Children were again matched according to functional abilities. Water races ranged from those with children swimming to those with more severely disabled youngsters being pulled through shallow water by counselors.

It is interesting to note that no matter how inactive a child was when being assisted by counselors, he was seen as the active racer or competitor. Although the outcome of a race between youngsters being pulled through the water by a counselor actually depended upon the performance of the counselor, this interpretation was never observed. Counselors became extensions of wheelchairs or were seen as a means to an end; the children were considered the actual competitors.

Certainly for the severely handicapped children themselves, they were actively involved in such races for they experienced the sensations of racing, though it was not actually their physical ability which counted.

In talking with children and observing these two events where children were grouped by functional ability, it was clear that the children enjoyed them. While each participant seemed to be trying his best to win, competition was not the main emphasis of these races. Campers shared the value of the staff members that each person get a chance to participate and thus did not boast about winning or complain about being matched against someone of a different age or sex. There was no complaining about unfair rules which prevented some of the more able children from winning all the time.

Grouping campers according to functional abilities was not common, however. Practically, it presented problems and required long, tedious hours of work for staff who had to prepare team assignments. Judging functional ability of each camper was extremely difficult, for in many cases what a child could do and could not do was not clear.

In addition to the practical difficulties of grouping by functional ability, there was a hesitancy on the part of camp personnel to do so. It required openly differentiating between children. Counselors found this a difficult requirement and some said they could not tell some children that they were not able to participate in various activities.

Toward the end of our fieldwork we relaxed somewhat our rule about not interfering in camp activities, and suggested that the more able-bodied children might help in the dining hall. At the time, counselors had been serving food and clearing up after meals. The following exchange shows the dilemma faced by the counselors. Some favored giving extra responsibility to the more able children, while others disliked the idea of "discriminating" against the more handicapped.

Assistant Director: There was a time when no kitchen girls were in the dining hall. The counselors went to the window and got the food and capable campers were allowed to carry it, until you'd see someone with both thumbs in the milk pitcher. After a while we decided that this wasn't a good thing. Then they could still take the dishes back, but it became a question of who could and who couldn't.

Rick [counselor]: You are developing a distinction right there. *You* can do it, but *you* can't. You are saying, "You are more able; therefore I am going to give you a privilege." It's work, but these kids think it is a privilege.

Ed [counselor]: I want to say something to Rick's point about saying to some people you can do it while to others you say you can't. I bet they get that all the time. They get it at home and it is ridiculous if you think you are pulling the wool over the eyes of a kid who is in a wheelchair by telling him that he is equal in all activities. If they can scrape dishes, it won't hurt them and it also makes it easier on us. If they get a big kick out of serving, I think it is a really good idea.

Pete [counselor]: Why should I say to one of my kids, "Your only problem is sight. I want you to do this." Why should I give him this privilege and make everyone else suffer? Because you are going to come to the point where there are kids half way in-between.

Jamie [counselor]: Yeah, but there are lots of kids in third pool and you tell them, "You can't swim as well as the kids in the second pool."

Pete: He can work at *that.* But I'm saying there are the kids in the middle that I am going to have to say, "No, you can't do it." He'll say, "What about this other kid: why can't I do it too? Then what do you say to him?

Camp Director: What he is saying is this. I asked Larry [legally blind camper; oldest cabin group] to paint the walkway out in front of the craft cabin. He did a great job. Now, Henry Williams [cerebral palsy, crutches, spastic, retarded; oldest cabin group] every morning wants his paint brush. (group laughter).

Rick: What do you do?

Director: Well, I don't give it to him because I know that Henry would be lethal with a paint brush (laughter from group). So I have to tell him in a nice way, every morning, either that I can't find the paint or I lost the brush. I am getting to the point where I will have to tell him that I really don't think this is the job for him.

Ed: You should tell him that he can't do it. Tonight he wanted to take his bed down and we told him that he couldn't do it and he said, "all right", and we took his bed down for him. The fact that you tell Henry he can't paint the walk hasn't ruined his camp experience. Just tell him and then give Larry a little responsibility so that he can grow up a little bit.

Pete: It's just the in-between thing that bothers me. I don't want to tell a kid, "You know, you're a nice guy and you know your disability is not too, too bad, but I don't trust you to do this." Because there are people that you can trust and people that you can't trust.

Rick: Yea, let's say some breakfast we have hot cocoa. The kid, you know, can do it but the cocoa is just too hot and the kid spills it all over another camper. Now what do I say to that camper? That's my fault and I am not going to take that kind of responsibility.

Rachel [counselor]: I think one of the aims of this camp is to make them more independent so that they are able to go out and live as normal a life as possible. When they go out with normal people they are going to realize that they have limitations and they have to learn to accept these. I don't think we should harp on it, but if you tell them, I think most of these kids will accept it.

Rick: And, if they don't . . .?

From recorded counselor
meeting 7/17/70

In addition to the hesitancy to distinguish between more and less able youngsters, the consensus among counselors seemed to be that without the more functionally able children participating in activities, the type of activities offered would have to be greatly limited for the slower children. In other words, if the severely disabled children were placed together for activities, they would not be able to do much and the counselors would not be able to do much either. As a counselor expressed this idea:

> What would it mean if we had the more able kids together and the less able kids together? It would end up being just a babysitting job in the lower groups. It would be good for the able kids but who (which counselor) wants to just babysit for four weeks?

From interview 7/7/70

As the above statement implies, each counselor must have his own boundaries of preferred levels of performance in activity. Persons who seek jobs as camp counselors are a relatively healthy, active group and enjoy moderately high levels of physical activity themselves. Perhaps there is a range with some counselors not being as bothered by low activity levels while others would have less tolerance for it.

When faced with a passive group of youngsters in a setting where activity is the expected norm, there is an excessive burden on the counselors to assume the role of performers so that an acceptable level of activity can occur. It means that the counselors have to be giving, arranging, carrying, pushing in order that they and the children are not faced with the prospect of having nothing going on.

The work required for counselors when playing with active children is different from that required in providing momentum for a group of physically limited youngsters. The counselors at Woodland preferred the former type of activity and preferred to have able-bodied children grouped with the more severely disabled so that the level of activity could be relatively high.

Looking at segregated camps and integrated camps with an overview, the activity level at Woodland was lower than at the integrated camps and the counselor group was observed doing more entertaining, more pushing, pulling, lifting, arranging and providing the focus of activity. This was especially true when campers at the segregated camp were grouped by functional ability.

PARALLEL PLAY

A second type of programming offered to accommodate the physically limited child simultaneously with the physically active youngster was parallel play. This was a form of grouping by functional ability. The difference was that cabin groups remained intact; all children in a cabin attended the same activities together. Within an activity they were differently employed.

Members of a cabin attended crafts or boating or sports activity as a group. During the scheduled period, parallel tasks or games were set up so that children could proceed at their own speed and ability. In boating, for example, the camp had canoes, row boats, and a specially designed pontoon boat. Some children were wheeled onto the pontoon boat and taken for a ride while those who could do so learned the techniques of canoeing and rowing.

In crafts, those who could perform adequately to do intricate work such as making love beads or a lanyard were helped with such projects. Those who had limited movement could finger paint or partake in projects which only required gross motor movements. While some children spent an activity period playing kick ball, others could play bean bags or lawn darts.

Parallel play occurred daily during the entire camp period. However, there were difficulties encountered with this type of programming. Children tended to rank activities in order of preference. Valued activities became those participated in by physically competent youngsters. For example, making and wearing love beads was seen as desirable by all the children whether or not they were capable of stringing small beads. Since all the children wanted love beads, it was the counselors who made them for those who could not.

At other times the handicapped children refused to stay occupied with such an activity as bean bags. They preferred being allowed to play with the more competent children. Discussing the possibility of planning more parallel activities, a counselor summed up the problem this way:

> Let's face it, Sammy Kendall [wheelchair, involved arms, fifteen years old] isn't thrilled playing bean bags. After two or three times doing it, he isn't interested in throwing the bags through those holes. But when

we play kick baseball and we take his chair, and Burt Caseman [fifteen-year old, no hardware, slight motor involvement] pitches him the ball and we push him around the bases, he thinks that's great! He's thrilled by that. So, to some extent I think we are compromising so that everyone gets at least some stint at athletics, but it works. . . .

From group discussion
7/17/70

Although counselors and staff made an effort to offer parallel activities simultaneously for every level of functional ability, the children tended to reject those activities requiring little physical competence, preferring those enjoyed by the more able youngsters.

GROUPING BY INTERESTS

The variation of mental functioning and interests levels of the children presented some problem and although there were no formal programming attempts to overcome these differences, there was informal grouping according to interests. Among the oldest boy campers there were a number of campers interested in and knowledgeable about electronics. These three boys are often excused from other activities they did not wish to attend and were allowed to meet together in an empty cabin on the outskirts of the main campus.

They spent a great deal of time in Cabin Ten working on broken radios or discussing electronics with each other. They asked campers, staff and researchers for broken radios, tape recorders and the like which needed fixing. Some tools and equipment had been donated to the camp by one of the camper's parents and other needed tools were usually borrowed from the camp's maintenance staff.

This informal grouping by interest, however, only involved three campers who were considered mature enough and physically able to go to the cabin by themselves (there were a number of steps leading up to the front door) and remain there. It was considered quite successful by counselors, staff and the campers involved, although the main program of the camp did not include grouping by interests.

It is difficult for any institution to respond too much to the special interests of its members. Grouping by pre-arranged activities is more economical in terms of money and personnel. It is also more amenable to administrative planning, for example, budgeting, purchasing and arranging for space.

The grouping by interests at Camp Woodland described above was informal, spontaneous and pushed by the boys themselves. Interestingly, the camp responded positively, probably demonstrating more flexibility than the usual institution. But the staff had many reservations since they could not assign counselors to oversee the activity and were afraid for the safety of the children and the property.

The flexibility of the camp in allowing this spontaneous special club to develop is probably a reflection of their general philosophy of flexibility in rules to accommodate the individual needs of each handicapped camper.

ALTERING ACTIVITIES

The most common type of programming at Woodland Camp did not involve regrouping of children. Cabin groups played together and games or activities were altered to meet the needs of the severely handicapped and the less disabled at the same time.

It should be noted that Camp Woodland did not program strenuous sports. Such activities as tennis or horseback riding were not in the program at all. The director and his staff selected field activities which could be played with special equipment or easily altered. For example, kick baseball was played with a large enough ball to be seen by those with visual difficulties or hit by those with motor difficulties.

In addition to a selection of less physically demanding activities, it should be remembered that the physical properties of the special camp were designed to give the handicapped person more freedom of movement. Paths were black-topped, playing fields were flat and architectural barriers had been removed. The cabin areas were close to the crafts building, the lake and the athletic fields so that children did not arrive for an activity already tired by the effort of getting there.

Counselors helped the more disabled children play. In a game of kick-baseball, for example, when a child could not kick the ball and run, the counselor would kick the ball so that the child could be already on his way to first base.

For children with visual problems, a counselor or camper would catch a ground ball and give it to a blind child to throw into home base where another child would be calling, "Here, here!" to give an auditory cue.

It was common for more able children to play at less than their actual ability or even to fake incompetence. Both boys and girl campers were observed pretending to drop a ball or pretending to be tagged so that the more disabled children could get a chance to make a winning play. Whether or not the more disabled children perceived this bit of deception remains unclear. What was felt by the counselors and most campers was that such deception more than paid off in giving children the chance to help others.

Male Counselor: If there is a game of baseball and they have to compromise for the people, they kind of drop the ball and stuff like that. It's not being done grudgingly either. You know, maybe we do have baseball games when they get physically challenged. The other times when they don't get completely, physically challenged, like having to compromise for the wheelchair, they are doing it most of the time in such good spirits. What's being lost in physical challenge is being gained in a little bit of understanding. Like I've never seen a baseball game that's been a real drag. They do all they can to make it exciting for the wheelchairs and they know they'll get their reward.

From interview 7/6/70

Joan [camper, spina bifida, brace, motor involvement]: No, I don't mind slowing myself down for the other kids. I'm not the fastest kid, you know, and I know what it's like to be the slowest one all the time. It doesn't mean that much to me to win anyway, but to be able to give someone like Wilma [crutches, involved arms] the chance to come in first; that's okay.

From interview 7/16/70

Not only are the activities pitched to the level of the more severely involved children, but so are the values of the campers and staff. Children are expected to help others. True competition in sports is discouraged and the expectation is that children will help others, not compete against them.

There were few incidents observed of physically competent children resenting the fact that they could not play and compete to the best of their ability. If they felt angry about having to slow down, there was no overt evidence, even though they were observed and questioned about this practice in interviews. There were only two children who commented that they would have preferred going to a regular camp where, according to one, "They really play baseball." It seems more likely that resentment was felt against competent children who did not share the value of helping others.

There were some highly competent children present. These were the non-handicapped children of older staff members who brought their families with them to the camp where they were given cabins for housing. Staff children were in the camp program on a day basis. These youngsters ate and slept with their parents, but were expected to participate in the camp activities each day.

One reason some of the staff children presented a problem to the counselors was that they were often more competitive than the handicapped campers. The following incident occurred when the son of a staff member came up to bat in a baseball game being pitched by a totally blind camper.

> Walter [totally blind] was pitching and kept asking the catcher to talk so that he could tell where to throw the ball. Rick [counselor] was standing next to Walter making such comments as, "Get 'em up, Walt"; "More to the right, okay?" Walter usually threw the ball too close to the ground but most of the kids swung when the ball came anywhere within possible reach for hitting. Lew [staff son] came up to bat. He stood there and didn't hit and didn't hit and didn't hit and didn't hit. The ball was not pitched well enough.

> "Gee, what's he want?" Walter yelled.

> "Yea," hollered another kid, "That was a good ball; you should have hit it."

> A counselor finally called three strikes and Lew was out. He was

obviously mad, for the pitches were not really good ones.

From fieldnotes 7/10/70

The inclusion of staff children in the program caused enough bad feelings for the subject to be brought before the director and counselors for discussion. There was a question as to whether these children should remain in the camp program or be taken out. The following comment by a counselor to staff members shows that to him the problem was learning a new set of values:

> If their parents decide that they should be in the program, they can survive it. I mean, it will take a little tolerance and it will be different, but this isn't something that is born. I think it is developed. You can develop this tolerance in the staff kids and they would get this tolerance if they worked at it. They can develop tolerance by eating meals with us and see someone slobbering all over the table. You develop the tolerance I'm talking about, because I have seen some of my more able kids say at the beginning, "I won't sit next to *him*," and then they say later, "Yea, I will sit next to him and I will help him eat better and I will clean up after him."

From group discussion
7/17/70

When activities were altered to accommodate the handicapped children, they resembled activities offered at the integrated camps in name mostly. It was a belief among counselors that segregating the physically handicapped children made it possible for them to be given opportunities to participate in normal activities. It was believed that they were excluded from these normal activities the rest of the year, and segregation could provide them with as normal an experience as possible.

The rules and manner in which activities were performed were changed, special equipment was substituted, and the more able children often had to hold themselves back from full participation or feign incompetence. Although there was a pretense of keeping scores and competing, true competition was stifled and the value of winning was replaced by the values of helping and of exhibiting tolerance. Some of the effects on interaction between campers and staff brought about by the programming and the commitment to integration will be discussed in Chapter Eight.

PROGRAMMING IN
THE INTEGRATED CAMPS

IT is usual procedure in regular camps to group children by age. It is assumed that children of similar ages will enjoy doing similar things and be able to do them together, since youngsters develop physically and socially at approximately the same rate. At Camps Cherokee and Hiawatha, the programs differed from those at the segregated camp in that they were designed for non-handicapped children.

Counselors had to face the dilemma of leading groups of activities, however, for children of unequal abilities. Among the normal youngsters there were children who performed physical tasks competently; there were others who were awkward or uncoordinated physically. Some moved at a much faster pace than others. Among the normal children were youngsters whose interests differed from the majority of their cabinmates. The addition of five handicapped children in each camp also widened the distance between campers in terms of physical and mental ability.

Counselors were asked how their cabins functioned as a group. None felt that the children made a good grouping, and the different areas of functioning specified were similar to those pointed out by counselors at the segregated camps: physical ability and mental ability, including interests. Table VII shows these answers by counselors.

The counselors in the non-special camp faced the same conflicts in programming that those in the segregated camp faced: leading activities for children with different physical and mental abilities as well as different interests. Many attempts to resolve this conflict used by those at the segregated camp were tried by staff working at the integrated camps.

TABLE VII

CABIN COUNSELORS' IN INTEGRATED CAMPS RESPONSES TO THE QUESTION:
"DO THE CHILDREN IN YOUR CABIN MAKE A GOOD GROUPING?"

Response	*No.*	*Percent*
No, Not Entirely	13	100

1. Difference in Physical Abilities (7)

   "The problem is that Norman [CP, poor motor coordination, poor speech] is so much slower than the other children. And he talks so slowly, nobody wants to take the time to listen to him. Like when there's dishes and all that, the kids don't want him to help because he's more of a hindrance than help."

   "Fran [hydrocephalic, poor motor coordination] is picked on by the other kids a lot. They think that she can't keep up with them. They just don't want her with them if she can't go just a little bit faster."

   "It's difficult sometimes when we do things that Alex [post-polio, braces] can't do. It's hard to know what to do with him."

2. Mental Abilities (6)

   "It's harder for Vickie [CP, retarded] to catch on to anything that isn't straight forward, you know, like teasing which the kids like to do all the time. She doesn't get it."

   "Norma [CP, crutches], I'd say Norma is more mature. Because a lot of the kids' conversations center around boys, which she doesn't enter into at all. She dresses differently. A lot of the girls borrow clothes which Norma doesn't like to do."

   "Peter [normal] doesn't want to play anything anyone else does. If he wants to play something, it's something like hide-and-seek while the others want to play baseball. We've had some fights over what we're going to do."

GROUPING BY FUNCTIONAL ABILITY

Grouping children by their ability is a frequent practice in normal recreational and educational settings. It is easier for instructors and children to have swimming instructions with others on the same level, for example. Usually, if you have narrow age groups, it is assumed that children will be homogeneous in terms of skills and ability levels, so that a minimum of sub-grouping is required. When handicapped campers were mixed into the regular group of campers, there were some difficulties in grouping children by functional ability.

At Camp Hiawatha, swimming instructions were given to beginners in the morning. Other children had sign up activities, such as sports and crafts. In the afternoon, intermediate and advanced swimmers were instructed while others played. This arrangement was made with the assumption that younger children would have swimming lessons in the morning and older children would be taught in the afternoon since most children above ten years of age were intermediate swimmers.

However, one fifteen year old girl with cerebral palsy was unable to pass beyond beginner's level. Consequently, she spent most of her camp day with children much younger than herself. She swam with younger children and had regular activities with them also. There was also a handful of normal youngsters who, because their swimming ability was low, were grouped with children much their juniors.

At the boys integrated camp, swimming instruction was given to all members of a village simultaneously. Counselors helped the waterfront staff and were numerous enough for village groups to remain intact.

Another example of grouping children by their functional ability was observed when one of us accompanied a group of the oldest boy campers on a three-day overnight camping trip.

Before leaving together on a camp bus for the mountains, it was decided that there would be two hikes, one for the more physically competent boys, and one for the slower and less competent campers. Boys were given a choice as to whether they preferred to climb mountains during the day trips (the long hike), or remain at the base visiting tourists attractions in the area (short hike). Counselors made the ultimate decision, however, so that although the prestige of being able to go on the long hike caused some youngsters to sign for it, counselors assigned them to the short hike if there was any doubt about their hardiness.

Two handicapped campers were in this oldest village; one a boy who had had polio, and now wore a leg brace; the other a boy with cerebral palsy, with motor involvement. Both signed up for the long hike and both were subsequently assigned to the short one.

During the hike it was observed that while those going on the long hike had more prestige in the beginning for their superior physical competence, soon the short hike took on prestige because campers got to see famous tourist attractions the others were missing. By the end of the camping trip, it appeared both hikes were equally desirable. Here was a case of each hike having something of value for its participants.

GROUPING BY INTERESTS

At the boys' and the girl's integrated camps, children were assigned activities according to their interests. At Camp Cherokee the youngsters designated their preference for activities when they first arrived and then were assigned to activity periods according to their interests and village group. Campers could choose between such activities as archery, riflery, crafts, boating, basketball, tennis, baseball, nature or sailing. Those choosing archery, for example, were scheduled with other youngsters from their own or a neighboring village.

Children interviewed for this study were asked what they liked doing best at camp. Among normal campers, preferences were fairly evenly distributed between swimming, boating and canoeing, riflery and field sports. Handicapped children also had a distribution of preferences. Interestingly, three of the five handicapped boys chose baseball as their favorite activity, the camper with an arm amputation, another who was slow and often short of breath because of a congenital heart condition and a third camper with cerebral palsy resulting in motor impairment. The remaining two Easter Seal youngsters preferred archery and swimming.

Activities offered at Hiawatha changed daily. Those listed for the day were pre-planned by the head counselor in conjunction with counselors who would lead them. For example, a day's offering might include: crafts, story telling, trampoline, nature, sand modeling, scavenger hunt, volleyball, tennis, boating, and newspaper. There were two activities in the morning, one in the afternoon.

A bugle call woke children each day and those dressed first were allowed to leave their cabins and go sign up for the activity of their choice. The main bulletin board was located at the bottom of the hill about a minute's run from the youngest campers' cabin and a two minute run from the oldest girls' cabin.

But there were a limited number of spaces to sign up under each listed activity. Once an activity was filled, campers had to select from the remaining ones. Such an activity as crafts always closed relatively early for it was extremely popular. If a girl chose the same activity too frequently, she was discouraged from continuing to do so in several ways. The counselor could tell her not to sign up again for a number of days. She could also be reminded that at the close of each camp session, awards were given to campers who selected a variety of activities.

After a bell was rung indicating the end of rest hour after lunch, the rush to the bulletin board once again began, with children wanting specific afternoon activities. The youngsters with mobility handicaps were observed to be among the last to sign up. The deaf child who had no trouble running, was highly competitive and prided herself on getting to the board first.

In some instances, handicapped children were given special admittance to activities which closed early if they had not attended for awhile. Most frequently, they signed their names below those activities the others had not chosen, thus having relatively little say in what they would do.

When asked what they liked doing best at camp, most non-handicapped girls answered crafts. Others mentioned liking to swim, trampoline, and singing in that order. Among the handicapped girls, two preferred swimming; one liked crafts best and one mentioned trampoline. A youngster with cerebral palsy and slightly retarded said that she liked writing letters home best. Among the ten handicapped campers interviewed in the integrated camps, she was the only one whose preference did not match those of the normal youngsters. The other Easter Seal children liked to do the same things although their physical limitations often resulted in poorer performances.

Since it was assumed that all children were within a normal range of ability or that with a little bit of help the handicapped children could participate in all activities, there was some concern among the counselors when they were faced with children of limited physical abilities.

The following incident shows how surprised a counselor was when she realized that some of the children could not go along with her activity plans despite the fact that they had signed up for it. Ruth was the nature counselor and she had planned a birdwatching hike where the children were to be taken into thick woods. While on their hike, she planned to point out different bird songs and calls. Two children with physical handicaps, both using crutches, signed up for birdwatching (or were forced to sign up because other activities were closed).*

> *Ruth* [counselor] : I blame myself. I hadn't been expecting them. I was planning to go across the street and then up and around through the woods. It was my first activity, you know, and all of a sudden I didn't know what to do. Who would have thought that some children couldn't walk. Thank heavens you [researcher] were along. I was able to leave the girls with you at the bottom of the hill. I see now that that's a typical problem where you have kids who can't do what the rest can do, but I still don't know what to do.

From interview 7/6/69

As this and other counselors learned, children's interests were not necessarily correlated with their ability to perform. As the data suggest, the handicapped children had the same interests as

---

*It is important to note that no explanation was given about activities beyond listing their titles. Children mentioned signing for some activities without knowing what was involved. In the above incident, it is conceivable that the handicapped children thought birdwatching was a relatively inactive event involving sitting.

their non-disabled peers. They wanted to participate in activities and signed for them regardless of whether they could perform well or even in the usual way.

Counselors, when faced with the discrepancy between the demands of an activity and the ability of some campers, handled the situation in a variety of ways. They suggested at times that the handicapped child go do something else. Or, they asked the child to just watch. At other times, they attempted to create special roles for the child with a disability. The counselors also attempted to help the individual to perform well enough to be included with the other players.

SUPPLEMENTING CHILD'S PERFORMANCE WITH HELP

As the *commitment to integration* suggests, each child was to be seen as an individual and helped according to individual needs. (See Chapter Six for a fuller explanation of this philosophy). At times children were brought into an activity because of counselors' assistance which, in effect, brought the child's effectiveness within the normal bounds of the game.

Two examples occurred. First, a handicapped girl signed up for trampoline. She wore braces and used crutches. The counselor, at first put off by her signing up for trampoline, later helped her to enjoy it.

Counselor: I don't really know why Babs [hydrocephalic, braces, crutches] signed up for it. I mean, trampoline is a pretty popular activity; it's usually filled up right away. She must have really scrambled to get to the sign-up board.

At first she just sat there and didn't want to do anything. And, uh, then I said, "Hey, Babs, how about getting on with me?" She got onto the trampoline and sat there, and I said, "Uh, hold your legs, clasp them to you." I stood in back of her and bounced her up and down and she really had a great time.

And she was really good; better than most of the kids; more alert at things like guarding and keeping upright.

From recorded group
meeting 7/8/69

A male counselor comments on a child with a physical handicap being given special help:

I had Ken [congenital heart condition, poor muscle tone] for archery. He didn't have much strength to pull back all the way on the bow. I let him have the easiest bow and then let him stand a little closer to the target. I don't think the other kids minded, and when he hit the target, we all cheered.

From interview 7/18/69

While the two previous incidents were successful examples of helping a child, only certain activities lent themselves to such a resolution. If the activity were arranged for children to take turns or work on individual projects as in crafts, it was possible for counselors to give individual help. They readily did so.

If an activity was so structured that teams of children were competing against one another, it was difficult to assist. If each child's performance was tied to that of the other participants, counselors' help tended to be considered unfair and was resented. Or, the game was no longer "for real."

Normal campers would help at times when a handicapped camper came up to bat, but this was resented by other campers. When Norman [cerebral palsy, motor involvement] came up to bat, the members of the team shouted to the pitcher to stand closer and throw the ball slower so that Norman could get a hit. Such help was not given readily and it was often reacted to negatively.

Normal Camper: I think we were playing softball today and he (Norman) [cerebral palsy, motor involvement] was on one of the teams. He kind of, you know, took the spirit out of the game. Um, that's understandable, of course, but we couldn't really play because we had to help Norman and the teams weren't really even with him, you know, on one.

From interview 7/19/69

Or, for another example:

Counselor: The kids got into a real hassel today about David [arm amputation]. We were scheduled to play in a game of baseball and the kids were upset. In front of him they said that it was unfair that

David was on their team.

From interview 7/18/69

Among 123 normal campers at the boys' camp, there were five children sent by the Easter Seal Society. Among sixty-six normal girl campers, five were physically handicapped. Counselors were willing to help handicapped children when possible, but they were not willing to have the majority of campers play a game at less than their ability. This would go against their philosophy of offering a normal camp experience for all. In like manner, there was much pressure from the non-handicapped campers to play games as they were "supposed to be played." Boys wanted to play baseball and were intolerant of changing the game to accommodate one or two slow, incapable players.

Occasionally in games being arranged on an informal basis by campers themselves, rules were altered to accommodate a handicapped child, but in such cases helping the physically disabled camper was the object of the game. In scheduled activities, games were conducted according to accepted rules given in rule books.

There were situations when counselors felt that there were no ways a child's performance could be brought up to standard. The discrepancy between a child's physical ability and the demands of an activity were so great, it was assumed that the child could not participate.

Female Counselor: I didn't know what was planned so when all the kids got into a circle, I said, "Come on Norma [cerebral palsy, crutches], join hands."

Then Alberta [counselor leading dancing] came to me and whispered, "We're going to do the Hora and I don't think she'll be able to do it." She whispered it to me and I don't think Norma heard.

So I said to Norma, "Why don't you sit in the circle, sit down and, you know, watch everyone do it."

She said, "Okay." She just sat in the circle. Then someone said, "Well, we're going to be kicking. We might kick her. Why doesn't she sit in a chair?" So I said, "Why don't you sit in a chair, Norma?" She said, "Okay."

From interview 7/6/69

The above example not only shows how the handicapped child was asked to remove herself from the activity, but also how counselors tended to deal with such children indirectly. Norma was never told directly that she could not participate; rather the group leader whispered to another counselor who asked her to sit elsewhere. At times when it was felt that youngsters could not participate in a planned activity, they were asked to leave the area altogether.

A number of incidents were observed when children with handicaps were left with the nurse in the infirmary while the rest of the cabin members played an active game assumed to be too difficult for the child. In commenting on this practice, counselors said that they did it because it would be unfair to both the normal and the handicapped child to have him stay.

It was unfair to require normal children to slow themselves down to accommodate the slow-paced camper. It was also unfair for the handicapped child to have to watch, "eating his heart out" while normal children played a game he could not play. The counselors decided that it was better, periodically, to remove the physically handicapped youngster from the group entirely.

Games were competitive activities and counselors as well as non-disabled campers preferred to play them in the traditional way. Counselors helped children with disabilities in order to compensate for their lack of physical competence. If children took turns or worked on individual projects, counselors' help was possible. However, in team efforts when each child's performance was linked to that of others, non-disabled children reacted negatively to their game being altered to accommodate a slow player. Handicapped children also disliked being held responsible for holding up an activity.

CORE AND PARA ROLES

When children with different abilities were scheduled to play team activities, there were attempts to devise roles for children who could not participate in the usual way. These positions, such as cheering at a baseball game or beating a drum during marching, most often evolved spontaneously or were assumed by a handicapped child with enough aggressiveness to do so. A male counselor talks about playing baseball with his cabin group which included a boy wearing braces:

Male Counselor: It's hard when you're playing baseball to figure out how Alex [post-polio, braces] can fit in, you know. He couldn't stand up at bat or run around in the outfield. He began coaching at first base. It sort of happened all of a sudden.

He was just sitting there and there was a close call. We asked his opinion and we agreed with what he said. He kept calling then, although once he called a runner out. Everyone else said that he was safe, so they just let it go that he was safe.

From interview 7/18/69

As another counselor's comment shows, such alternative or *para roles* were not always well accepted.

Counselor: The idea of his being a referee is fine but the guys didn't need one. He was the umpire at baseball, but not really, because they didn't need one. He knew it too.

From interview 7/18/69

There were real or *core roles* and pseudo or *para roles* when it came to a sport such as baseball. Roles and performances involved in any but the core activity were not as valued by the campers and when, in the above incident, they did not agree with the umpire, they disregarded what he called.

It is easiest to see the ranking between core and para activities in relation to the boys' camp where competitive sports were stressed more.*

The same phenomenon was observed at the girls' camp where there was a literal interpretation by counselors of how activities were to be performed. For example, when two girls wearing braces and using crutches signed up for marching, they were asked to

---

*Both the boys' and girls' integrated camps in this study were relatively non-competitive in their approach to camping. While some camps emphasize competition on an individual and group basis, those chosen by the Easter Seal Society for placement of physically handicapped campers were not particularly competitive. Competition, of course, is to be expected in a normal camp where children play team sports.

leave by the counselor in charge. Marching was seen as walking around in time to music and since the children were unable to walk well, it was assumed that they could not march. The activity marching was not conceived by the counselors to include having an audience or beating a drum.

The most frequent group functioning at the integrated camps was to have all children play together whenever possible regardless of their abilities. Sometimes the less capable child was assisted to meet rule requirements; sometimes they were given para roles and sometimes they were excluded because it was assumed that they did not fit in.

COMPARING PROGRAMS

Regardless of which camp employed them, counselors said that basic differences among campers affected their functioning as a group. These differences among children were categorized in terms of physical abilities, mental abilities and maturity of interests. Counselors and camp personnel had to resolve the question: How to program for groups of children with a wide variance in functioning levels. The solutions offered at the integrated and segregated camps were sometimes the same and sometimes different. The difference can be understood partly in terms of camp philosophy and partly in terms of the demands of the more capable children.

A commitment to segregation shared by those working at Woodland Camp led to the expectation that children *should* participate in all activities. This required a flexibility in programming whereby rules were stretched or made up on the spot to accommodate each child present. This expectation resulted in the frequent use of game modifications since everyone, even the most severely disabled children were accommodated. Children were expected to help each other, not compete with each other.

The commitment to integration shared by those at Camps Hiawatha and Cherokee led to the expectation that every child *could* participate, although at times some youngsters with disabilities might need counselors' help. In actuality there were times when counselors could not help because normal youngsters resented the fact that the games were being changed in the process. There were also times when the discrepancy between the handicapped campers' ability and the requirements for a game were felt to be too great.

In summary, some techniques were used by both types of camps to resolve the conflict of having different levels of ability within a group.

METHODS OF PROGRAMMING EMPLOYED AT CAMPS

I. *Regrouping children, while keeping normal, traditional rules*

1. *Parallel play* such as baseball and bean bag game during athletics period. Two games are played simultaneously.

2. *Creating alternative or para roles within a game.* Such as having one child be umpire while others play ball. One game is played and performers assume different positions within it.

II. *Changing rules while keeping original grouping of children*

1. *Slight modification* such as making exceptions for one or two players and having pitcher move closer to batter.

2. *Major modification* whereby rules for all players are changed such as using large volleyball to play "baseball".

While it appears that there was more grouping by interests at the integrated camps where campers were asked to sign for their preferences, this was actually allowing children to pick from the offered schedule. Campers at the integrated camps did have more responsibility for their own programs in that they got to select what they wanted. Campers at the segregated camps were assigned activities.

In addition, at the segregated camp, children were accompanied at all times by counselors who were responsible for taking them to activities, stayed with them, giving them help when needed to maintain the level of performance of those involved. Children at the integrated camps were responsible themselves for getting to and from activities and were expected to be there on time.

The value of competition was underplayed at the segregated camp and replaced by a value of helping others. Whenever possible children were expected to help those physically less able. Performances in a game such as baseball were homogenized with the more able children holding back or pretending incompetence, thus placing themselves on a par with the more handicapped players. At the integrated camps, the activities were often competitive. The slow or handicapped children were frequently the weakest members of a team or asked not to play at all.

The philosophical approach toward the handicapped child and the actual programming of each camp had significant effects upon the campers themselves and the social interaction which occurred, as we will describe in the next chapters.

Chapter Nine

VALUES AND SOCIAL RELATIONSHIPS IN THE SEGREGATED CAMP

THE social structure of each camp, as well as the philosophical views shared by camp personnel, had an effect on the grouping of children, their friendship networks and the types of relationships children and staff experienced.

It was understood that every child in Camp Woodland had some physical handicap. This fact alone promoted an awareness and openness concerning physical defects which was not observed at the integrated camps. At the segregated camp there was less need to pretend normalcy by hiding one's disability or managing relationships so that the other interactants might be kept unaware of a handicap. As a matter of fact, having a handicap was one's ticket of admission to Woodland Camp and many instances were observed where children were openly discussing their disability, showing how a wheelchair worked or asking others what it was like to use crutches.

In contrast to the usual denial of disability, it often appeared that there was total openness concerning handicaps in the segregated setting. This was not the case. While much talk centered around handicaps, there were some campers who did not join in these conversations and some types of disabilities, such as colostomy bags, were never discussed.

Counselors were instrumental in fostering talk about handicaps in that they frequently asked youngsters whether they could use a disabled arm enough to carry a ball, or how they thought they might do a project in handicrafts given their poor ability in fine motor movements. Since the social structure was arranged so that every child was to participate, games could be changed to accommodate a child once he or she made it clear how he or she could participate.

In the case of hidden or unusual handicaps, if it was not clear to a child what was wrong with another camper, he or she might ask. The following excerpt shows how children openly discussed their disabilities.

> I was sitting at lunch when the kids from Cabin Two [approximately 12 years old] started discussing Linda [cerebral palsy severe mental retardation, slight motor involvement]. Jenny [legally blind] asked Patty [counselor] what was wrong with Linda. Patty's answer was as follows: "There is something the matter with Linda's brain but it's not the same as with somebody like Alice [CP, motor involvement]. Alice also has brain damage but it affects her legs and arms only. With Linda, a different part of the brain was damaged and it affects her ability to think. It's not her fault that she doesn't understand too much. That's just the type of cerebral palsy she has."
>
> Jenny seemed satisfied with the answer and said she was glad she wasn't like Linda. Jenny and the others at the table who were listening to the conversation started discussing their own handicaps with each other. Zelda [legs perthes] explained that she didn't have cerebral palsy at all. For the next ten minutes, the kids were trying to decide who had CP and who didn't.

From fieldnotes 6/24/70

HANDICAPS: THEIR MEANING TO CAMPERS OF DIFFERENT AGES

Youngest Campers

As could be expected there was a progression in the sophistication of talk about handicaps as the children advanced in years. In the two youngest cabins, with boys and girls aged six to ten years, there was much curiosity about one another's defects, but there was a lack of understanding as to the meaning and implications of having a handicap.

Although the children themselves had experienced their own physical deviancy, in observations and interviews they seemed unaware of any far-reaching implications these might have on their lives. Each, in his or her own fashion, had learned to cope with the necessities of life as best as possible. The concept of living with another type of handicap possessed by cabinmates was a matter of curiosity. Among one or two of the oldest girls and boys in these groups, however, one could see a growing understanding of the meaning of their handicaps to others.

One ten year old girl who had two colostomy bags which had to be changed regularly by counselors was taken into the counselors' quarters for this process. Both counselors and the camper appreciated the privacy of the separate room. While she had learned to change one colostomy bag herself, Pauline needed help with the other and expressed both embarrassment and emotional discomfort at having others involved with her in the process.

For the most part, however, children remained on the level of merely recognizing others' differences and in some cases even expressed jealousy of secondary gains others had. Several cabinmates of the girl with the colostomy bags stated that they wished they were Pauline and could be taken into the counselors' quarters too. Each child when interviewed was asked whom he or she would like to be most. The following excerpt shows the lack of understanding behind the younger children's reactions to handicaps.

Interviewer: If you could be anybody in camp, who would you want to be?

Rose: [albino, vision difficulty, aged 8] : Pauline!

Interviewer: Why Pauline?

Rose: 'Cause I like to ride in a wheelchair (laugh) and I know how to push myself, too. Pauline gets a lot of attention.

Interviewer: Would you mind it if you had to stay in the wheelchair all the time like Pauline does?

Rose: I'd love it!

From interview 7/16/70

Even with further probing there seemed little understanding of being wheelchair bound other than that it meant getting to ride around. Among the younger campers there was delight in introducing fellow cabinmates as, "the boy without a hand" or, "This is Vanessa; she has to wear casts all night long." With the maturity which comes with growing older, children seemed more aware of the total picture of the lives of handicapped people.

Middle Years

Handicapped youngsters in the middle cabins (aged ten to thirteen years) were less open about handicaps with strangers and each other in terms of staring and curiosity or envy. There was a much greater tendency to understand feelings of others and even to imply feelings that went beyond the dialogue or present action. Children did not talk negatively about children in front of them, although they did talk behind their backs at times. These observations can be understood in relation to Flapan's (1968) research on children's understanding social interaction.

In her study of children's ability to perceive or to make influences about feelings, thoughts, and intentions, and of their ability to interpret or explain sequences of behavior that occur in interpersonal relationships, Flapan found that the most conspicuous developmental increases occurred between children aged six and nine years, suggesting that this period represents an important transitional phase. She suggests that her study supports the findings of Piaget in relation to the concept of egocentricity. According to Piaget, older children are more capable of viewing situations from the standpoint of the other person.

Aware of others' feelings, the campers in the middle ages shared experiences with each other and enjoyed play-acting together. The pre-adolescent girls enjoyed many hours of informally playing hospital.

> Although I only observed the girls in Cabin Two playing hospital twice, Patty [counselor] told me that they play it over and over again. The game usually begins with two or three girls taking the role of patients, hospitalized and needing an operation, usually on the legs. Several of the girls were doctors and nurses. The amount of

knowledge of medical terms, both instruments and parts of the anatomy are surprising, but perhaps only to someone who has not spent time in hospitals as these children have. Other children take the part of parents and relatives visiting the patients. Karen Douglas [severe mental retardation, gargoyle features, little speech] and Cathy [autistic, slight motor involvement] were usually included in the game. They were the distant cousins dragged along with the parents for the visit.

From fieldnotes 7/12/70

Oldest Campers

The oldest campers, thirteen to sixten years, shared experiences with each other such as stories of hospitalization and surgery. Among some of the more mature girls the level of understanding involved discussing life styles and working out together future possibilities and difficulties. The older children had more experience with normal children by virtue of age alone. They were concerned about such events as marriage and child bearing. Some discussions were on the conceptual level of being handicapped as well as sharing personal feelings about their own problems.

In the oldest girls' cabin, there were four teenage girls who were particularly close during the summer. All had been to Woodland Camp previously and they continued their friendship from one year to the next. The four enjoyed spending free time together and were usually observed in deep conversation. The following excerpt from fieldnotes describes one rap session briefly and the level of their concern with their own and each other's handicaps:

While the rest of the cabin group watched movies in the cabin, this rainy day, Joan [spina bifida, leg involvement], Elaine [epilepsy, grand mal], Jayne [cerebral palsy, slight motor involvement], and Ruth [arrested cancer, leg amputation] were sitting out on the porch with Betty [counselor] involved in deep conversation. I realized today how familiar this scene is. The four are always together. Overheard pieces of their conversations reminded me of my college days where such soul-searching sessions are commonplace.

Betty [counselor] was saying that she was in favor of euthanasia. She explained how her father, a doctor, often came home with stories about somebody who, although a vegetable, was being kept alive with modern drugs.

All the campers disagreed with Betty. Each said that they were against mercy killings, for "who knows, we might have been the ones killed." Thereupon ensued a discussion of suicide. None of the four girls felt that they had ever wanted to kill themselves or die. Joan said that even if she were more limited than she was, she would want to live.

This led to a discussion about whether they might feel differently when adults. Again, each said "no" although Elaine admitted she was fearful as to whether she could have children. She and Jayne feared that their children might also be handicapped, and Elaine was primarily worried because of her epilepsy, and whether she could give birth safely.

The conversation was interrupted by the ringing of the lunch bell and as they started walking toward the door, Betty was saying she had never thought about the implications of euthanasia; she had always pictured older people in the terminal stages of a painful disease when discussing it.

From fieldnotes 6/10/70

The openness about physical handicaps and the fact that children could talk to others about their own hospital experiences contributed to the positive feelings many campers had toward the segregated camp. When asked if they would have preferred attending a regular camp, a frequent comment of campers was that they liked being in a special camp better for it provided them with the opportunity to talk to others like themselves in addition to the chance to learn ways of managing.

Interviewer: Would you like to go to a regular camp? [Camper attends regular school.]

Millie [cerebral palsy, crutches] No, because I get to see friends with my own problems and it's easier to cope with mine. I can see that I am making it and you see how much better you are than some of the other kids, and it's really fun talking to others who have the same problems you have.

From interview 7/16/70

Or, in the case of a fifteen year old girl:

> *Interviewer:* Would you like to go to a regular camp? [Camper attends regular school.]
>
> *Joan* [spina bifida] : No, I think it's easier to learn in a group like this. I have some very close friends here and I can talk to them. I don't know about anyone else but I can really express my feelings here. I think it is different in school because a lot of your problems are with other kids.

From interview 7/16/70

FRIENDSHIPS: QUALITY AND QUANTITY

Although difficult to document, it was felt by the researchers that friendships at Woodland Camp were deeper and closer than those established by handicapped children at the integrated camps. Impressions and observations were based on several facts. Children dealt more directly with each other at the segregated camp, and while there was some laughing and talking behind others' backs, there was a minimum of this behavior at the special camp. A large amount of joking about the handicapped campers occurred at the regular camps. It is important to point out that several aspects of the social structure of this special camp lent themselves to the formation of closer friendships.

The camp session was four week periods instead of two week periods as at the regular camps. There was a high return rate for campers and counselors alike; 63 percent of the counselors interviewed had worked at the camp before and 78 percent of the campers interviewed were returning for at least their second year. Campers and counselors knew each other from previous sessions and could build friendships upon this past knowledge.

Woodland Camp was coeducational. Without exception, when asked how they would like the camp if it were not coeducational, counselors and campers felt that the camp would not be as "good", "as much fun", "as meaningful a summer", or as "normal and healthy a situation". There was an ease and friendliness between girl and boy counselors and campers with the two oldest cabins getting together periodically for a teenage party. On the beach and while waiting for meals, children of both sexes could be observed laughing and kidding one another.

Counselors especially emphasized the importance of having male and female staff at the camp. Some dated each other on off hours while others formed friendships with members of the opposite sex which involved a lot of helping with such things as lifting heavy objects and special tasks as sewing buttons.

The camps being coeducational seemed to contribute significantly to the warm relationships between campers and counselors and for many this was a necessary element for their accepting work there.

Another factor leading to closer relationships may have been the rule that campers remain in cabin groups for all activities except swimming and special programs. Children spent their day from cabin clean-up to programmed activities, dinner and evening events with the same twelve to fifteen youngsters and five counselors. Contacts with non-cabin members in the camp were fewer than at the integrated camps, and this provided more opportunity to get to know those in one's cabin better.

When children were asked who their friends were at camp and why they liked them better than other children, the handicapped girls at Woodland reported having more friends (Mean 2.8) than did their counterparts integrated into the regular camps (Mean 1.6). On the other hand there did not appear to be much difference between boys who were integrated (Mean 3.0) or segregated (Mean 2.7). Normal girls claimed many more friends than handicapped girls in either camp, though there were no such differences among boys.

It is interesting to note that while at least one handicapped child in each camp studied said that they had no friends, none of the normal campers claimed to be completely friendless.

At all three camps studied, three reasons for being friends were stated most often: personality traits, frequency of contact, and shared interests.

We wondered if choice of friendships among these handicapped children was related to the severity and type of children's disabilities. When asked why they liked their best friends, children stated that they chose them on the basis of personality, frequency of contact and shared interests. But there does seem to be a correlation between friendships and disability since seventeen out of thirty-two children (53%) indicated their best friends had the same disability as they and of similar degree of severity, a finding beyond chance.

Among campers with motor disabilities, children either chose friends with similar disabilities or less disability than they, except for two cases. One camper with motor involvement which required no braces, crutches, or prosthesis chose a friend who did need hardware, and one child wearing braces said that his best friend was in a wheelchair. Four out of eight campers with vision difficulties named others with sight problems as their best friends.

Besides picking friends who were similar to them, there was an indication of symbiotic relationships. In a few instances, children with quite different handicaps formed a friendship which seemed functionally beneficial to both. A case in point was the close and frequently observed friendship between a totally blind boy and a camper with severe cerebral palsy confined to a wheelchair. Holding onto the back of Micky's wheelchair, Walter walked all over camp, helping to push when there was a hill or obstacle in Micky's way. Micky mentioned Walter's help as one of the reasons he liked him better than any other camper.

Interviewer: Why do you like Walter [totally blind] best?

Micky [CP, wheelchair] : I know he can't see, but he did a terrific thing for me. He helped me put my shoes on, helped me get dressed. We just get along great together. He walks up to dinner with me and everything. And, we just like each other.

From interview 7/11/70

In like manner a girl with hearing difficulty shared a close friendship with another girl camper confined to a wheelchair who had severe speech involvement. While Frances was unable to move about and could not talk with others, she could converse by pointing to letters on her lap board and loved to play checkers. Carol [congenital deafness, motor involvement] could move slowly on her crutches, but had difficulty talking and hearing. It was a familiar sight to see Carol making her way over to Frances' chair where the two, with the use of the lap board letters, would talk or play checkers.

MANAGEMENT TECHNIQUES

The fact that children at Woodland Camp indicated they had more friends than the handicapped campers at the regular camps, and that these friendships were deeper and more intense is not to suggest that management techniques were absent from this type of social structure.

Especially in the early days of the camp session, children could be seen staring, pointing, or talking about certain obvious or unusual disabilities with each other. Getting adjusted in the special camp meant learning how to deal with everyone's particular limitations. With some of the more involved or retarded children, relationships never moved beyond the state of limited, managed dealings.

As Goffman states, "Social settings establish the categories of persons likely to be encountered there" (Goffman 1963, p. 2). It was expected that everyone had a physical handicap and if a child complained about another, he was likely to be reminded that there was something wrong with him, too. The task of orienting oneself to the segregated camp was not to discover who was different, but rather how they differed and how to deal with children of all descriptions, capabilities and personalities. As one researcher described her reactions:

> I find myself quickly learning what each individual child can do. Although we have been at Woodland only a few days, I find that this small corner of the country is the world; the boundaries of the camp immediately formed the boundaries of my world view. In a setting where some children can't speak at all, atonal, slow, halting speech is close to normal. Quickly one learns to interact with everyone, and initial discomfort is covered by jovial conversation.

> For instance, Big George, the very large-headed boy with hydrocephaly and mental retardation, is "Lover George". He likes to take people by the hand while rolling his eyes. He kisses the hand saying, "You're my girlfriend; you're my boyfriend." This is Big George. This is what he does and very little else. So when I see him, I say: "Hi,

George, am I your girlfriend?" And you see that everyone greets him this way. "Who's your new girlfriend, George?" It's impossible to know what goes through George's mind, but you can have contact with him and know what to say when you find yourself sitting next to him.

Or you see Hugh Williams who can't talk at all, very spastic and in a wheelchair. He is probably one of the most severely handicapped children in camp and you learn when he is shaking his head "yes" and when he means "no". And you learn what makes him smile, so you remind him that you saw him win a race yesterday, and he grins happily shaking his head in a movement you've learned means "yes". While walking away, you hear one of the campers also mention the race to him.

When Cathy, who is autistic, gives you a smile or reaches for your hand, you feel real contact and you feel as if this is a relationship; all is right with the world. The bubble bursts, however, when you leave for a few days and then, upon returning, have to get re-oriented.

From fieldnotes 6/29/70

The fact that a child has a handicap is no guarantee that he will feel positive, helpful and cooperative toward other disabled children. One teenager asked to leave camp after two weeks because he found it depressing to be with the other handicapped children. He was one of the few campers to mention being upset by handicaps. We looked for other signs of negative feelings about physical handicaps and thought there might be an excess of teasing. However a noticeable aspect of the camp was the minimal amount of teasing between campers. It was discouraged by counselors.

There was teasing at the camp, but there were only six or seven children toward whom teasing was "allowed" by counselors.

The children teased frequently were among the most disabled at the camp. Most of them were also severely retarded and did not respond with obvious hurt or anger to the teasing; they responded with giggles or other non-aggressive responses. Perhaps in the face of severe disabilities and retardation, laughing and teasing were needed for release of the tension, anger and depression inevitable to some extent in a camp with over 100 physically handicapped children. Those children chosen as targets were judged to be safe ones.

Karen Douglas, a severely retarded thirteen year old girl possessed the most objectionable looking disability at the camp. Her condition left her with gargoyle facial features, large eyes and a distorted mouth and nose. Her tongue was perpetually hanging from her mouth. Karen was one of the campers frequently teased or laughed at.

> Sitting at the lunch table next to me today was Ben [counselor]. He spent a good ten minutes telling the other staff members how he got Karen to give the peace sign. While talking about her, Ben tried to get her attention so that he could show the others how, with eyes bulging, tongue hanging out, Karen formed her fingers into the V for victory sign, grinning from ear to ear. Everyone at the table laughed loud enough for others to turn around. They began to see if they could get her to give them the peace sign.

> From fieldnotes 6/29/70

> There is no doubt that Karen Douglas has the most grotesque features and deformity at the camp. Yet, it is always she who is being kidded and laughed at. At the Christmas party, it was Karen who was asked to do the kooch-koochy dance in front of the entire group while everyone laughed.

> From fieldnotes 7/30/70

As a counselor working with Sammy Kendall [severe cerebral palsy, overweight, wheelchair, involved speech and sight] stated it: "to laugh sure helps." Sammy was a fifteen year old, badly disabled boy who had little use of his muscles. Sitting in a wheelchair, his chest rested on his knees except when he was helped to sit straight. To help move him at home, his parents had had to purchase a special lift. His speech was difficult to understand, yet Sammy was universally popular among the girls as well as boys. He was tickled, teased, kissed, and talked to. As a counselor described it:

> He gets so much, so much teasing. We prod him about how the girls are so attracted to him. It makes it easier truthfully; it makes it easier

for the counselors to tolerate it, if you can do a little teasing, really, we've talked about it. Sometimes we'll use a little vulgarity or something and it might not always be real desirable, but it really makes it easier on the counselors if you can loosen up a little bit and you can say, "You fat slob." I don't know why it is, but someone like Sammy, he's great but you have to tease him.

Like the other night at 2:30 in the morning. I hear him calling my name and I came out and I had to turn him on his side and powder his butt. It's much easier if I can say, "Big fat thing, why can't you do it yourself?" and start laughing and he starts laughing. I mean sometimes you get so tensed up with this stuff, it's impossible not to.

From interview 7/8/70

When interviewed Sammy said that he really did not like the constant tickling, although he appreciated it as friendliness on the part of others and enjoyed the attention. He rejected the suggestion that he tell the counselors not to tickle him because it would hurt their feelings.

Laughing at or with these children helped manage relationships where the disability was particularly upsetting. On the other hand, we saw the relative lack of teasing behavior in general between less disabled children and counselors as a reflection of the camp's value system. Helping others and cooperation between participants was encouraged; competing against one another was not favored behavior. Teasing, a form of making fun, did not fit into the social system.

VALUE SYSTEM

There was an optimistic attitude toward being handicapped at the camp fostered by the fact that there were so many activities for all to participate in. The stereotype of the lost, lonely, disabled child sitting alone while others ignored him was absent at Woodland Camp. And there were many stories of children who had never gone swimming before or who had never played baseball who were now swimming or had hit a homerun. According to some children's interviews, camp was indeed the highlight of their lives.

During the winter because he lived on an isolated farm, one boy spent most of his time watching television from morning until night. A number of children were visited a few times each week in the winter by a home tutor but this was the extent of their interaction with people outside the immediate family. A young girl arrived at camp with braces too small for her because her parents had never had them checked. It was at Woodland Camp that the girl took her first step. There were many heartwarming stories about the camp infused with a positive feeling about coping with handicaps.

A highlight of the season was a Christmas-in-Summer party. The dining hall was decorated, campers gave a skit, and Santa Claus arrived with his bag full of toys. Santa Claus, a traditional visitor, was the camp cook, who was appreciated by campers and staff alike for his loving attitude and generosity toward the children. The Christmas party, thought to be important for the children who did not receive presents on December twenty-fifth, meant each child got a gift of his or her own at camp.

It is not surprising that eighteen (75%) of the counselors interviewed stated that a camp like Woodland gives the children opportunities they wouldn't get elsewhere. In part, their response reflects the spirit of optimism and hope present in the camp's atmosphere. It reflects a feeling that Woodland provides a special place for physically handicapped youngsters.

Camp therapies played an important part in this general atmosphere also. It was through speech, occupational and physical therapy that the disabled children could hope for, and actually experience, improvement. With only one or two exceptions, the campers liked the therapies and worked hard while there. Specific advancements, some rather dramatic, could be seen during the summer. When a child who had been confined to a wheelchair took her first steps, the news traveled throughout the camp.

Emphasis was on helping others and cooperation among campers and staff. When campers, usually at the beginning of the camp session, complained about someone else's handicap, they were reminded that they, too, had a handicap. The social system stressed cooperation. A song written by two boys reflected this value system. It was written to be sung to the tune, "This Land is

My Land" and was sung by its authors during lunch on the first parents' visiting day:

My Hands Are Your Hands

> My hands are your hands
> Your eyes are my eyes
> God made them for me
> To share with you.

Chorus: Oh, God made them
> Oh, yes he made them
> Oh, yes he made them
>   for me and you

> You give me your sight
> I'll give you my touch
> And we can work it
>   for all of us.

Chorus: Yesterday was a bad day
> Today's a good day
> for Woodland campers
> like me and you.

From fieldnotes 7/5/70

COUNSELORS' RELATIONSHIPS WITH CAMPERS

Counselors' familiarity with the youngsters resulted in a possessiveness and protectiveness of them. There was a camp rule which stated that children must always be accompanied by a counselor. When youngsters were attending an activity and it was time for a cabin member to go to therapy, a counselor took him there and later returned to pick him up. Children were accompanied by counselors to the dining halls for meals and to the beach for swimming, and if during the free period a group of children wanted to pick berries in the woods, they had to find a counselor willing to go with them.

A large degree of control over the behavior of campers was

maintained by this requirement that campers never be left alone. Each camper's whereabouts was always known and how they behaved was under constant surveillance. As a result, counselors were familiar with each child's abilities, physical and mental. While this aspect of the counselor-camper relationship resulted in campers having little or no responsibility for themselves, it also gave children freedom of movement that they might not have had if they were with adults less familiar with them.

Some children using crutches and with poor motor coordination fell frequently, yet counselors were not unnecessarily concerned about their getting hurt. Campers were encouraged to run back and forth when possible. Children who had always been helped when making their beds at home were taught and required to make them by themselves at camp, although given their ability it looked like an impossible task. Counselors took certain campers in swimming who a stranger might assume should not be taken into the water. Some had never been swimming before attending Woodland.

Counselors' helping behavior toward the physically handicapped children was most often with the goals of the child in mind. Ladieu, Hanfmann and Dembo (1947) in their excellent article concerning help and its meaning to handicapped persons point out how non-disabled persons frequently give help to expedite matters, while help to a handicapped individual frequently means assistance that is essential to the attainment of a goal.

When making her bed, a handicapped child did not want counselors' help except when she was unable to lift up the mattress enough to get the sheet under the corners. Although it took Alice [cerebral palsy, motor involvement] 45 minutes and required a great deal of physical effort for her, she preferred doing it alone and improved over the summer.

Assistance to the handicapped individual makes learning difficult for them. Rather than being helped, such a person actually is restricted in his possible area of movement. In this way, a person who gives help is, in effect, depriving the handicapped person of the possibility of advancing toward independence and stronger self esteem.

Often, help extended by non-disabled persons to handicapped

individuals is an asymmetrical social relationship where the disabled person is placed in a lower status position. There is a lack of recognition of the handicapped person's existing abilities and an implication of pity. While the help-giver may feel virtuous about such giving, the handicapped individual often is stripped of self esteem and freedom.

In many ways the social structure of the special camp and the counselors' attitude and familiarity with campers resulted in a shared definition of help whereby children were encouraged to do as much as possible for themselves.

The pace of the camp allowed a child to be slow, so that taking 45 minutes to make a bed did not result in a child's being late for morning activities. In the regular camp, where time allotted for cabin clean-up was shorter, a handicapped camper was constantly being asked to hurry with her bed since she was expected to be on time for early activities.

It is important to distinguish between helping a child try and develop new ways of coping, and giving a child the *responsibility* for himself or herself. While the constant control of counselors at Woodland over the campers resulted in a great amount of freedom of movement for the children, it also resulted in campers having little responsibility for themselves or their actions. When one is constantly under the care of another person, there is little need to make decisions and assume self-responsibility. Campers at Woodland did not have to worry about getting to the right place at the right time for activities. They were taken there by counselors.

During field observations, it became quite noticeable that campers had little interest or idea about future events. If a camper were asked what was scheduled for the afternoon, the usual response was, "I don't know." There was little opportunity for children to be in the care of themselves, for it was a requirement of the camp that they be accompanied by a counselor at all times.

There was an exception to this rule that campers had to be with counselors at all times. Three of the oldest campers who were specifically interested in electronics were allowed to meet together, alone, in an empty cabin to work on old radios, repair broken equipment, or talk together. However, other campers were not given this responsibility for themselves. There was a hesitancy to discriminate between campers with high and low functional abilities which resulted in counselors planning activities for campers as one group. Since there were youngsters at Woodland Camp incapable of assuming responsibility, counselors did not want to give responsibility to some while denying others.

To eliminate the need to discriminate between individuals and still maintain control over 123 handicapped campers, counselors stayed with the children constantly and kept them playing together. This resulted in the need for individual performances having to be equalized so that everyone could participate as a group. It was expected that campers would cooperate and help each other when necessary. Since the value system in the special camp made cooperation the valued type of behavior, children showed little resentment when a teammate's performance resulted in the team coming in second.

There was little observable evidence that campers hesitated to include the more disabled children on their team. Winning was not important; helping was. In like manner, when the more able-bodied youngsters compromised their own performances so that slower campers would be able to play or even make winning moves, there was no evidence that this was done grudgingly. The opposite seemed to be the case. Those children who were *able* to compromise their performances could also pride themselves on their ability to do so and could enjoy the implied acknowledgement of their physical superiority despite the fact that they were not winning.

Four older girl campers, generally acknowledged to be the leaders of their cabin, indicated this feeling of superiority by words and actions. They were standing together in front of their cabin kidding one another while the rest of the cabin was being organized into two games of shuffleboard. The shuffleboard games were painted on the blacktop in front of their cabin and the athletic director, Frank, was organizing teams.

Elaine [epilepsy] Look who Frank put together: Wilma [CP, crutches] and Judy [CP, crutches] .

Jayne [CP, slight motor involvement] : We'd better go help. I'll go on Judy's side and you (indicating Joan) go over to the other side.

From fieldnotes 7/4/70

True competition was minimal and therefore campers were not motivated by a desire to perform better than others or to be the best. Campers who shared this value of cooperation seemed to make an adjustment in camp easier than children who were more competitive.

Chapter Ten

VALUES AND SOCIAL RELATIONSHIPS IN THE INTEGRATED CAMPS

THE expectation for children at Camps Hiawatha and Cherokee was that they *could* participate in all activities. While staff and counselors were well aware that some physical tasks were difficult for children with physical handicaps, they felt that these youngsters could be assisted so that their abilities would come within the normal range. Once faced, however, with the actual campers and the practical problems of leading group activities for children with a great variety of differences, it was seen that giving individual help was not always a reasonable solution.

COUNSELORS' RELATIONSHIPS WITH HANDICAPPED CAMPERS

Since much of the responsibility for the success or failure of individual activities fell upon the counselors, there was a tendency for them to maintain control over games and players. Campers were consulted on what games they wanted to play, but how these were to be played was not open for discussion. It was assumed that games could be run according to widely accepted rules. To ensure that these activities were played *correctly,* counselors tended to pre-judge the handicapped campers' ability to perform. They made their own evaluations of the ability of the handicapped youngster before an activity occurred and did so without consulting the child.

Once it was decided, by the counselor, that one or another of the children *could not* and *should not* participate (because if they did the other players would have to compromise their game) the child was either told to leave or was indirectly excluded. The point is that relationships between the staff and handicapped campers involved dealing with each other indirectly. Handicapped campers were not asked, in most cases, what they were able to do or how they thought they might participate.

Medical records and an Easter Seal information folder was kept for each handicapped child and counselors had access to these. Counselors did not consult these records. Some felt that they should not for that would unnecessarily prejudice them about the child's capabilities. Staff could discuss disabled children with their camp directors, nurse, or Easter Seal representative, but they did so infrequently. The child himself was seldom consulted.

The avoidance of such direct confrontation with the handicap reflects, in part, the philosophical approach, *commitment to integration,* which involves treating all children alike and not emphasizing the fact of the disability.

When non-disabled campers asked the handicapped children about their braces or crutches, counselors often stopped the conversations, assuming that such directness would be upsetting to the handicapped individual. Had the counselors opened themselves up for the handicapped campers to tell them what they wanted to do and how they might participate in certain activities despite their physical limitations, there was the possibility that games and sports would have had to be altered to accommodate the slower players.

One cannot afford to ask individuals to help conduct an activity if he or she is not prepared to relinquish some of the control over the event. Control over scheduled activities rested with the counselors, the normal campers, and the traditions of society which dictated the right and wrong way to play games.

In like manner, it was the staff and counselors who decided when a handicapped child was trying to use his disability as an excuse to "get away with something". In this manner, the counselors decided what the child could do and avoided doing, such as clean-up activities in the cabin. Again, the observed fact was that the children were not asked directly or reprimanded directly. The counselors would tell campers what to do or when they were not trying hard enough, although the blame was not linked to the physical handicap, not openly at least.

Norma, a 15 year old girl with cerebral palsy, was noticeably slower than other girls in her cabin. How to include her in cabin clean-up was a problem for the campers and counselors in this group. Youngsters cleaned their own areas first, making their beds and straightening their shelves. Once these duties were finished, they consulted a schedule posted on the wall which showed each girl's cabin task for the day. Duties such as sweeping, cleaning the wastepaper basket, or picking up paper from around the cabin rotated among cabin members.

At the beginning of the camp session, Norma asked others to help her make her bed (a difficult task for her) so that she would have enough time to perform her cabin duty. Her counselor told the rest of the cabin group that there was no need to help Norma, that she could take advantage of such help and not learn to do things for herself. By the end of the two week session, Norma was responsible for her own area only, her name had been removed from the cabin duty schedule.

Interviewer: How about Norma?

Susan [14 year old normal camper]: No, because well, you see, Justine [counselor], she knows Norma takes advantage of her. Norma, well, Norma would ask her to do something for her, and all the kids, she'd ask them to help her up the stairs when she can do it herself. And, Justine won't pay any attention to her. She won't let Norma do that. Justine tells us not to do anything for Norma because then Norma won't learn to do it herself.

Interviewer: What does Norma do when nobody helps her?

Susan: She just goes and makes it herself.

Interviewer: Does she take very long?

Susan: Today I was walking outside when Norma was starting to make her bed. Most of the kids were at church and I made everyone's bed who wasn't there. Norma was the only other person in the cabin and she thought I was going to make her bed, too. She was waiting for me to make it.

So when she saw me walk right past her out of the door, she just started making it herself. And then about 40 minutes later when I came back, she was still making her bed, just finishing it. I guess it does take her a long time.

From interview 7/6/69

Later when interviewed, it became apparent that Justine, Norma's counselor, had a physically handicapped mother. Her assumption that Norma did not really need help or should be made to do things herself can be seen in direct relationship to her mother's injury, a lower leg amputation caused during a World War II bombing raid in London.

> *Justine:* I feel a bit annoyed with Norma sometimes, more because my own mother is physically handicapped. She was wounded in the war as a young woman before she met my father. She does everything, whereas Norma. . . . I keep thinking, well, I'm sure it's just because she's not allowed to do it, and if only someone would allow her to do it, she could do it.
>
> And, you know, I think this is what annoys me more than her actually not being able to do it. I keep thinking that there's something at home or somewhere, or if not, let's work to find out what's holding her back.

From interview 7/9/69

Most counselors did not base their judgements on personal knowledge of other handicapped persons or relatives. Faced with the fact that handicaps were not discussed openly at the integrated camps, and that the disabled children were rarely consulted about their own physical limitations, counselors were left to base judgments of them on early impressions of the campers, their own fear of disabilities or folk knowledge of physical deviation.

Among the staff members there were some who felt that the handicapped campers should be given preferential treatment. These adults tended to give the disabled youngsters more favors or to discipline them less. As the following illustration shows, counselors could be unaware of their special handling of handicapped campers.

Female counselor: You see the trouble with Babs [hydrocephaly, crutches] is that she is so cute. When she looks at me with that freckled face and those big blue eyes, leaning on her crutches, I give in to her every time.

Interviewer: Did you ever discipline her?

Counselor: I guess not but I didn't realize it until the other kids picked it up. They came to me and asked me, "If Babs is bad, would you punish her too?" They didn't like that I was protecting her.

From interview 7/8/69

The following excerpt from an interview with a male counselor, points up the difficulty counselors had in deciding how to treat the handicapped child.

Neil [counselor]: From the day Norman [CP, motor and speech involvement] arrived, I was worried about him and had a tendency to always look after him. I figured the other guys could take care of themselves, but Norman had to be watched. Mark [counselor] had a tendency to say, "well, I'm going to treat him just like I treat another camper," so a couple of times right at the beginning when he didn't do what he was supposed to do, Mark said, "C'mon, Norman!" a little bit angrily.

I didn't think that was right. Since then, I think probably we sort of hit a medium between that. I feel that he can't be a regular camper but we're not going to really spend a lot of time looking after him. He's got to learn to look after himself, partly because we don't have enough time.

From interview 7/19/69

The data suggests that in the integrated situation where only five out of approximately one hundred children were handicapped and the desire was to "overlook" the handicap and keep it from becoming an important part of a child's identity, it was the handicap itself which caused such children to receive preferential or negative treatment. Often unfamiliar with handicaps, counselors attempted to deal with them as best they could while working with the non-handicapped children simultaneously.

The disabled children perpetuated this situation of indirect interaction. They reacted according to their assessment of what others expected of them, and did not directly state what they could do or assert themselves upon the social group. The handicapped children held themselves back until "permission" was given for them to join in group activities. They were on guard against being excluded, and when asked to leave, there was never any protest.

In *Deviance Disavowal: The Management of Strained Interaction by the Visibly Handicapped,* Fred Davis (1967) suggests that the physically handicapped person may develop special techniques for moving past the initial tactfulness and distance they are likely to receive upon first acquaintance. They attempt to move to a more personal plane where in fact their defect will cease being a crucial factor. Davis calls this process *breaking through.*

Observations in each integrated camp were for two weeks, the length of a camping session and the length of time these children and campers lived together in camp. In this amount of time, while there were slight changes observed between certain of the handicapped campers and specific counselors, the overall impression was that relationships between them did not develop significantly. The die was cast early in the camp period whereby counselors and handicapped campers were to deal indirectly with each other, managing their relationships so that the fact of the handicap was not dealt with openly.

CAMPER-CAMPER INTERACTION

In the integrated camps there were subtle forces preventing the segregation (or sub-grouping) of the handicapped children. According to the philosophy of committment to integration, handicapped and non-handicapped were considered alike as individuals.

The staff either unaware of the sensitivity of the handicapped children to each other or at a loss to know what to do about it, gave the children no encouragement to acknowledge each other as having similar problems.

In certain cases children felt that another handicapped camper was their best friend although they were not together often.

Interviewer: Who are your friends at camp?

Norman [CP, motor involvement]: Alex [post-polio braces], because he has something the matter with him just like me.

Interviewer: Well, why do you like him?

Norman: I don't know. I just like him. Alex is handicapped. In a way, he's just like me.

From interview 7/18/69

A number of the non-handicapped children were drawn to the handicapped children. When pressed as to why they chose these children as their best friends, the reason was often linked to the existence of the disability. A handicap can mean many things to different people. In the illustration below, Laura, the non-handicapped girl, was under emotional strain because of her divorced mother's impending marriage to a man Laura did not like.

Interviewer: Who's your best friend?

Laura [normal, 9 years old]: Um, Babs [hydrocephaly crutches].

Interviewer: Why?

Laura: Um, because sometimes she has reasons to cry and I feel sorry for her. The girls always say she has to make her bed by herself, and when she doesn't know how. She has many reasons why because she has crutches and can't stand up.

Interviewer: Do you feel like crying sometimes, too?

Laura: Yes.

From interview 7/6/69

An important question to raise here is which non-handicapped campers were attracted to the handicapped children. As the above illustration shows, the projected sadness of a girl requiring the use of crutches was appealing to the girl quoted. There were other instances observed where non-disabled children who were emotionally disabled or who were socially rejected by peers were attracted to youngsters with physical disabilities.

Not all friendships between non-handicapped and handicapped children were contingent upon the fact of the disability, nor were all non-handicapped youngsters who chose handicapped children as best friends necessarily disturbed. The frequency of choice by non-handicapped campers of the handicapped individuals as best friends was not unusual considering the number of handicapped children at camps.

At Hiawatha, non-handicapped children mentioned one or another of the handicapped campers eight times when listing best friends. This represented 12 percent of the 57 names mentioned. Actually, handicapped children represented 6 percent of the camp group.

At Cherokee, the handicapped boys were mentioned 10 percent of the time when non-disabled youngsters listed their friends at camp. At Camp Cherokee, handicapped children represented 4 percent of the total group.

Handicapped children were chosen by others as friends but the handicapped children at the integrated camps reported having fewer friends than did their normal peers and those disabled children at the segregated camp. Handicapped girls at Camp Hiawatha usually named only one youngster when asked who their friends were at camp. Normal girls mentioned four children most frequently. The handicapped boys mentioned having two friends most often, as compared to five others being counted as friends by the normal children.

To summarize, handicapped campers seemed to feel more

friendless in the integrated camps, although the non-handicapped children felt friendly toward them. Often, though not always, this was an emotional reaction to the crippled condition of the handicapped child, reflecting identification with the presumed suffering of the handicapped person.

Several dimensions of the handicaps represented in this study are important in respect to relationships between handicapped and normal youngsters.

Hidden or visible. Two campers with hidden disabilities were at a disadvantage in making friendships. Ken [congenital heart condition] was slowed by his disability. He could not keep up with others without shortness of breath, and on chilly days he could not go swimming when other boys were required to do so. Ken was seen as odd, a baby, or the counselor's pet. His differentness was attributed to personality by boys who did not know of his handicap. The following excerpt is from an interview with one of Ken's cabinmates:

Interviewer: Of all the kids in your cabin, who don't you like?

Stu: [normal, eleven year old] : Um, I don't know his last name. Ken. He's a big lazybones. He's a brat. I tell him he has to go swimming like the rest of us even if it's raining and he says, "No I don't. Ask the counselor." He's a big baby, like on the overnight to the Navajo Village. He said, "Every time I walk along, I get real tired." So he got a canoe ride; we all walked along while he rode in the canoe, but we yelled at him the whole time.

From interview 7/19/69.

In a social setting where handicaps were not often verbally acknowledged, visibility helped acquaint the non-handicapped child with the limitations of such campers.

Acquired at birth or in later years. The time of acquisition of the handicap was important in several respects. Of the girls in this study, all had disabilities acquired at birth. Four boys had acquired their handicaps after birth, although one was only eighteen months old and had no memory of himself without crutches and braces. Children who acquired their disability after five years of age not only had a memory of themselves without the handicap, but also valued such competitive sports as baseball or basketball. This had both a positive and negative effect on two boys, both with amputations.

Steve had lost a lower leg a number of years ago. He had been fitted with a lower leg prosthesis and had learned to walk and run with it. When fully dressed, he could keep pace with his peers and competed well with them. When swimming, the prosthesis was removed and many youngsters stared at him, but Steve was a strong swimmer and won several water races, bringing glory to his cabin group.

David, had only recently lost his left arm. He was displeased with his arm prosthesis and chose to wear nothing most of the time. He also had knowledge of himself before the accident and valued excellence in performing sports. In his case, David expressed a great deal of anger against the non-handicapped boys and felt himself at a definite disadvantage.

Both David and Steve valued the same competitive sports as their non-handicapped peers and could appreciate the latter's feelings towards them. David, however, learned to evaluate himself negatively and Steve had been able to keep his self-concept as positive with the use of his prosthesis.

Norman [CP] acquired his disability in an auto accident at age seven. Subsequently he had been taught to judge his performance in terms of his own disabilities, not in comparison with other children. In so doing, he tended to be left out of those activities the normal children performed because he couldn't keep pace with them but expected them to compromise for him.

Severity of disability. All of the handicapped children in the integrated camps were able to care for themselves and walk to and from their cabin to the camp activities although they were slower. The pace with which they functioned had a direct effect on relationships between children. Handicapped campers in most cases were slower physically, mentally, or in speech. Counselors and campers alike found themselves torn between keeping pace with the normal children or slowing down for the handicapped ones.

As the following excerpt shows, a non-handicapped girl was torn between the requirements felt necessary to maintain a friendship with a handicapped child and the requirements of staying with the rest of the children.

At Camp Hiawatha, activities were sometimes scheduled to take place in The Grove. The Grove was a peaceful, wooded area with benches surrounding a cleared area under the shade of pine trees. To get to The Grove, each person had to walk down a relatively steep hill to the main athletic field, walk across the field and then up another rocky, irregular hill.

Handicapped campers mentioned avoiding activities that they knew were going to be held at The Grove because they felt guilty if one of the non-handicapped children walked with them and they were both late. They disliked arriving for the activity after it had already begun.

> *Laura* [normal camper, aged 9]: This morning I was standing and talking to Babs [hydrocephaly, crutches] in front of the main cabin. We were waiting for Chris [counselor] to tell us where we were supposed to meet for nature. When she arrived, she said we were to go over to The Grove.
>
> Before I knew what had happened, the kids rushed off leaving Babs, me and Chris. When she saw all the kids running off, Chris said she had to rush so that there was a counselor there when the kids arrived.
>
> I didn't know what to do. I said, "Babs, we'd better hurry." I guess she didn't like that 'cause she started to cry. I just left her alone and ran over myself.

> From interview 7/6/69

Severity of disability was important in the development of friendships in its effect on pacing and ability to perform, for when faced with a choice between joining with the more normally paced youngsters or slowing themselves down to keep pace with the slower individuals, most campers chose the former.

Shared Interests

While the pace with which one performed was a factor in the acceptance of the physically handicapped children by their peers, having similar interests was also important. Within a few days of the beginning of a camp session, specific interests emerged within each peer group which affected social contacts. Older girls campers in the same cabin (13 to 15 years) discussed boys that they had known at home or would like to meet in the future. Joking or discussing boys became the thing to do and being in with the group often depended on the degree of adherence to this interest.

Preadolescent girls (9 to 12 years) were concerned with practical joking and kidding one another. Younger boys (7 to 10 years) were sports-oriented, spending hours talking about the games they and professionals played. The social pressure to show interest in these areas of concern were strong and those not doing so were left out and often rejected.

Handicapped children were not the only ones faced with the problems of being accepted. Normal children were also excluded on the same basis of not conforming to the peer group interests, but the handicapped child had the added problem of not being *able* to participate.

Within one cabin at the girls' camp, there were two Easter Seal children, one was deaf and the other had cerebral palsy with slight mental retardation. The latter was placed in a cabin with children two years younger than she, but she was still unable to understand a great deal of the kidding and joking. She was generally excluded from the group.

The deaf youngster had a quick understanding of practical joking and was often a leader herself. As a matter of fact, this child turned her disability into an asset. By teaching her cabinmates sign language, they were able to have secrets while "talking" in front of counselors. Secret communication was age relevant.

While a youngster of a certain age may be excluded by peers at one age, the same child may be better accepted at a later time in his or her development when the disability is less dysfunctional with peer interests. Handicapped adults have more control in picking friends who share interest areas with them. Partly because there is a greater variety of permissible roles and behaviors for adults than there is for children.

Fran, a child who was well accepted by peers, was rejected repeatedly by older children. Fran [hydrocephaly, motor difficulty and deafness in one ear] was six years old. She had difficulty dressing herself, had to go to the bathroom frequently and did not hear well because of deafness. She was well accepted by children her age at camp. Many children in the youngest cabin had some difficulty with clothes. Verbal skills of six year old children vary and, for the most part, were not of prime importance in the development of friendships. Children at this age picked their friends by whose bed was next to whose, or because of general accessibility. Six year old girls seemed to like other girls who would go with them to activities or share toys. Fran had many friends among her own cabin group.

On the other hand, she was the brunt of jokes by older campers who teased her because of her awkwardness, both motor and verbal. Campers of all ages ate together at large tables in the dining room and Fran was required by some older girls to pass plates all the way around the table to the girls sitting next to her. She was laughed at because she frequently dropped food off her fork and preferred using a spoon for small vegetables. The fact that Fran often had to leave the table to go to the bathroom was amusing to them.

Another example of this point occurred in the oldest cabin group where a handicapped girl had different interests from fellow cabinmates. Norma [CP, crutches] was an average looking girl who did not enjoy spending time grooming herself or talking about boys. Her cabinmates spent a great deal of their time in these activities. Within the group, girls enjoyed sharing clothes and make-up. Norma did not participate in these exchanges. Her interests were reading, painting and "educational things." When asked what she liked to do best, she said, "I like to do quiet things; um, I like to read, paint, and do educational things."

The girls of the cabin organized a rap session. Each member of the cabin was supposed to stand up front so that others could criticize her. In like manner she was to discuss the good and bad points of others when they were up front. Norma did not actively participate, and her behavior angered a few of the more active cabin members. When interviewed, they complained about Norma's failure to go along with the group and take part in the things they did.

Near the end of the first two week camp session, a beauty contest was planned as one of the evening programs. Each cabin was asked to nominate a candidate and submit her name to the director. Three girls nominated Norma and submitted her name before the rest of the cabin could take a vote. The three were particularly annoyed by Norma's asexuality and intellectual airs.

Before the program began, the three were called to the director's office and admonished for their cruelty. "How," the director asked, "could they play such a cruel joke on Norma who would never be able to walk as they?" The girls were told to look at their legs and then look at Norma's legs and ask themselves how they could do such a mean thing to her. This was one instance (they were rare) were non-handicapped children were made to feel guilty about their own normalcy in relation to those with disabilities. Since Norma had already been told she was to be the cabin's beauty queen contestant, the director allowed the nomination to stand.

All three non-handicapped campers were extremely remorseful after their talk with the director and busied themselves helping Norma prepare for the event. They dressed her in their best clothes and spent time helping her apply makeup.

After walking around the room with the other beauty queen nominees, Norma was asked the question that each participant had to answer: What have you gotten out of camp? According to many, Norma gave the most mature and best answer. She said that camp was important to her for the opportunity it presented to someone like her to meet new friends, citing the three girls who had been so helpful in getting her dressed as a beauty contestant. None of the three attended the evening program but rather remained in their cabin.

Norma's mention of the three as friends was made with all sincerity. She did not display any feelings that she should not have been a contestant because of her handicap, nor that the three had been cruel to her. She did say that she was surprised to be nominated (surprised and pleased) since she didn't join in very many discussions with them.

Norma's asexuality was annoying to these girls whose interests had primarily to do with boys, dating and clothes. The friction between interests of these youngsters was strong enough to overshadow the fact that our society says one should be nice, not cruel, to handicapped persons. However, it is probable that when Norma enters an advanced age range and group interests change, she will be more accepted by peers whose interests are intellectual.

SEXUALLY SEGREGATED CAMPS

Both integrated camps were separated by sex. At Camp Hiawatha the staff hierarchy was entirely female with the handyman being the only male at the camp. There was talk about boys and boyfriends, but there was no actual interaction with members of the opposite sex. At Camp Cherokee, counselors and staff were men with one or two of the senior staff members' wives serving as arts and crafts instructors. At both camps, there was the attitude that one's sex was the best, and being completely self-sufficient (not needing any help from males or females) was praise-worthy.

At Hiawatha there was a pride in the competence of women without men which subtly pervaded counselors' informal discussions in off-duty time. Much of the energies and thoughts of the female counselors were spent discussing men.

Male counselors and staff at Cherokee enjoyed a male society comradeship. Boys were told how they "had better shape up or ship out." A few counselors at the camp tended to withdraw from relationships which emphasized male physical prowess and preferred a more sensitive, emotional relationship with campers. These counselors were frequently placed with younger boys.

SUMMARY AND DISCUSSION

Relationships and interaction between counselors and campers at the integrated camp tended to be less deep or direct than those at the segregated camp. Counselors *dealt* with handicapped children rather than interacting with them. They pre-judged the abilities of the children with the emphasis being placed on what they could not do, rather than what they could do. Since counselors were working with normal children primarily, the physical limitations of the handicapped child were a constant challenge for them.

In a competitive social setting where competitive sports and activities are being conducted, normal youngsters are themselves involved in maintaining a high level of performance. Each child, although perhaps a member of a winning team, had to maintain his individual performance or suffer rejection by peers. Befriending a handicapped child meant slowing oneself down to a pace acceptable to the disabled child. Non-handicapped campers did not often accommodate themselves to the slower pace. In this setting where physical prowess was emphasized, the handicapped camper was often left behind, asked to sit out, or forced into the group by counselors.

Commitment to integration implied that each child as an individual should be helped to be part of group activities. Actual observations showed handicapped children getting preferential treatment, being accorded superficial acceptance, or being excluded from core activities altogether.

At the integrated camps, it was believed that handicaps should be minimized as much as possible. The implication of this approach is that by overlooking them, physical handicaps will become unimportant, thus allowing the child to enjoy normalcy. While campers quickly learned that they were not to confront handicapped campers with questions about their disability, they talked behind the backs of the handicapped children. Campers with hidden disabilities were especially at a disadvantage for their physical difficulties were linked to personality traits.

At Woodland Camp where children were segregated because of their physical handicaps, talk and discussions were open and frequent. The children in both types of camp structures were constantly aware of their handicaps, although when they were talked about openly, youngsters were able to form closer relationships with each other and deal with the limitations imposed upon themselves and their interactants. At the integrated camp, the effects of the handicaps on interaction were not open for discussion or possible resolution.

At the segregated camp, the social setting was arranged to accommodate handicapped children with the result that many campers relinquished self responsibility. With the social setting arranged for them, they did not have to strive to fit in. With a value system that emphasized helping and cooperation, the handicapped campers at the segregated camp did not have to worry about the level of their individual performance.

Chapter Eleven

‱‱‱‱‱‱‱‱‱‱‱‱‱‱‱‱‱‱‱‱‱‱‱‱‱

SELF CONCEPT AND
SOCIAL STRUCTURE

‱‱‱‱‱‱‱‱‱‱‱‱‱‱‱‱‱‱‱‱‱‱‱‱‱

THE social structure of the camps seemed to affect not only social relationships among the children, but also their self concepts. Using a brief self concept test following our interviews with campers we found many differences not only between handicapped and non-handicapped children, but also between handicapped children in the integrated camps compared to those in the segregated camps.

THE SELF CONCEPT OF HANDICAPPED CHILDREN

Self concept has often been examined by personality and social researchers as a reflection of psychological strength or well being. Pitfalls abound in the use of measurement of self concept because it is purely a subjective state. It may be descriptive (I am a girl) or comparative and evaluative (I am too fat). It may be global self evaluation (I'm no good) or it may be specific (I'm no good in sports but good in school). But despite the difficulty in precisely defining the concept, there is considerable evidence that self concept is related to many types of behavior as well as to psychological adjustment (Coopersmith, 1967).

A positive self concept, often called self esteem, is correlated with more effective behavior. Whether the behavior comes first or the attitude comes first is often not clear. Behavior and self concept seem to influence each other.

Studies of physically handicapped children have generally concluded that these children's self concepts are more negative than that of normal children. (Krider, 1959; Richardson, Hastorf

125

and Dornbusch, 1964), and that negative self concept is associated with higher anxiety (Lipsitt, 1958). The more severe the physical limitations the more negative the self concept and lower the self esteem. The most severe effects seem to be in adolescents, especially adolescent girls who have physical problems of high impact and visibility. (Smits, 1964; Meissner, Thoreson and Butler, 1967).

Most comparisons of self concepts of handicapped and non-handicapped children have been done in public schools or other integrated settings, however. Breslin (1968), who studied handicapped children in special classes, could not find the expected negative relationship between self concept and severity of disability. The handicapped youngsters in segregated classes scored as high on Lipsitt's (1958) self concept test as did Lipsitt's normal group.

The implication from Breslin's work that a segregated setting may have a positive effect on handicapped children's self concepts is strengthened by Craig's (1965) findings that the self acceptance of institutionalized deaf children was significantly higher than either day school deaf or non-deaf public school children. Craig attributes this to the in-group feeling of the institutionalized.

MEASURING SELF CONCEPT

There are almost as many instruments to measure self esteem or self concept as there are studies of this topic. We found none in the literature that would be just right for our purposes, so we developed our own variation of an adjective checklist which we called by the tantalizing name, "The Like Me Test" (LMT). It is quick, easy to perform, and appealing to children six to sixteen. Even severely disabled youngsters could take the test, since it involved a minimum of communication and motor dexterity.

The LMT was given immediately following the interview which took place after the children had been at camp about ten days. A child was handed a pack of nineteen, 3 x 5 cards on which were written adjectives, one per card. He was told that the adjectives may or may not be like him. Would he or she please put each card in one of two piles: *Like Me* or *Not Like Me*? If the child could not decide, he could put a card in the middle. The adjectives were:

Mood:	*Social Competence:*	*Productiveness:*	
Happy	Friendly	Strong	Healthy
Sad	Lonely	Weak	Busy
Angry	Pretty (or Handsome)	Smart	Tired
Quiet	Plain-looking	Dumb	Fast
Noisy		Sick	Slow

The dimensions of mood, productiveness and social competence were, of course, specifically chosen for this study from a multitude of possible dimensions of self concept. We felt the effects of the different camp structures would most importantly be measured by concepts involving feelings of social and personal competence as well as general emotional state. From our pilot studies of children at integrated camps, we hypothesized that the children in this type camp would feel greater social pressures to compete and produce, but we did not know what effect this would have on their feelings about themselves. In the segregated camp we were interested in knowing if the special, more sheltered situation would lead to feelings of dependence and lesser competence, or security and greater competence.

We were able to use the LMT with some confidence because our pilot studies showed that the children accepted the test easily and test-retest reliability was high. However we could rely only on face validity that the test was measuring what we expected it to.

FINDINGS

The LMT was given to ninety-six children (Table VIII), ranging in age from eight to sixteen, with sex groups and handicapped and non-handicapped groups being of similar ages.

The test was analyzed by comparing groups of children according to the proportions by which they chose an adjective as *like them.* A test for significance of difference between proportions was used (Bruning and Kintz, 1968), and only those differences considered statistically significant are reported here.

TABLE VIII

CHILDREN GIVEN THE LIKE ME TEST

Campers	Boys Interviewed	Added*	Girls Interviewed	Added*	Total
Integrated					
Non-Handicapped	12	4	15	8	39
Handicapped	5	1	5	5	16
Segregated					
Handicapped	19	1	17	4	41
Total	42		54		96

*To enlarge the sample for purposes of statistical analysis we added some handicapped and non-handicapped subjects from the group of campers not interviewed and from another camp session. The added children differed from the interviewed groups in no discernible way in background characteristics or in LMT performance.

Age-Sex Differences

Considering the entire group of children, all ages combined, the choice of words as like them was similar for boys and girls. (Tables IX and X). The only significant differences were that more girls said they were *Busy* and *Tired*. This may reflect the strain of camp life on girls, compared to more physically oriented boys.

There were also age differences in choice of the words, and the age trends were slightly different for girls and boys.

Younger girls were significantly more likely than older girls to describe themselves as *Pretty*. They also more often said that they were *Tired*.

Younger boys compared to older boys more often chose the word *Handsome* as like them, as well as *Fast* and *Smart*.

These age-sex trends in children describing how they see themselves show the development of both modesty and a more self-critical attitude as children grow toward adolescence. Many children showed conflict about sorting the words *Pretty* (girls) or

TABLE IX

GIRLS' RESPONSES TO LIKE ME TEST
PERCENT OF HANDICAPPED AND NON-HANDICAPPED
SAYING ADJECTIVES WERE LIKE THEM

	Integrated		Segregated	
	H'c	Non-H'c	H'c	All Girls
LMT Adjectives	N=10	N=23	N=21	N=54
Mood				
Happy	100	91	95	94
Sad	30*	9	19	17
Angry	20	22	10	17
Quiet	80*⤢	39	43	48
Noisy	30	39	48	41
Social Competence				
Friendly	100	96	91	94
Lonely	10	13	29⤢	19
Pretty	90*⤢	48	52	56
Plain-looking	40	74*	67⤢	65
Productiveness				
Strong	50	70*	81⤢	72
Weak	40*⤢	9	10	20
Smart	70	83	71	76
Dumb	30	13	14	17
Sick	10	17	29⤢	20
Healthy	90	91	91	91
Busy	80	87	86	85
Tired	50	48	33	43
Fast	40	70*	71⤢	65
Slow	50*⤢	22	19	26

*Significant differences between Integrated Handicapped versus Non-Handicapped.
⤢Significant differences between Integrated Handicapped versus Segregated Handicapped. All differences noted are significant (p < .05) using a test for significance of difference between two proportions (Bruning and Kintz, 1968).

TABLE X

BOYS' RESPONSES TO LIKE ME TEST
PERCENT OF HANDICAPPED AND NON-HANDICAPPED
SAYING ADJECTIVES WERE LIKE TEAM

LMT Adjectives	Integrated		Segregated	All Boys
	H'c N=6	Non-H'c N=16	H'c N=20	N=42
Mood				
Happy	83	100	95	95
Sad	17	13	30 ≠	21
Angry	0	13	20 ↗	14
Quiet	33	31	45	38
Noisy	17	31	45 ↗	36
Social Competence				
Friendly	100	100	85	93
Lonely	33*	6	25 ≠	21
Handsome	50	56	55	55
Plain-looking	83 ↗	63	55	57
Productiveness				
Strong	67	75	65	69
Weak	0	6	35 ↗≠	19
Smart	83	81	70	76
Dumb	0	0	10	5
Sick	0	0	25 ↗≠	12
Healthy	100	94	85	91
Busy	50	69	70	67
Tired	17	13	35	24
Fast	17	75*	60 ↗	60
Slow	67* ↗	6	45 ≠	33

*Significant differences between Integrated Handicapped *vs.* Non-Handicapped.
↗Significant differences between Integrated *vs.* Segregated Handicapped.
≠Significant differences between Segregated Handicapped *vs.* Non-Handicapped.

Handsome (boys) and *Smart.* They seemed to feel restrained from publicly complimenting themselves on these dimensions (beauty and intelligence), demonstrating the development of the value: modesty.

Self Concept of Girls

Did physical handicaps in the girls studied affect their self concept, as other studies suggest? We found the answer to be yes if we compared handicapped girls in Camp Hiawatha with their non-handicapped campmates. But we found no differences in self concept between handicapped Woodland girls compared to non-handicapped Hiawatha girls.

Eight of the nineteen words were chosen significantly differently by the handicapped and non-handicapped girls at the integrated camp. The handicapped girls reported more negative mood (more *Sad,* and *Quiet*) and less feeling of productiveness (more *Weak* and *Slow,* less *Strong* and *Fast*). Although it would appear that they felt more socially competent (more *Pretty,* less *Plain-looking*), the age trends in girls showed *Pretty* to be more likely used by younger girls, and so its use by the handicapped girls may be a sign of social immaturity or defensiveness rather than competence.

In contrast to these results, the handicapped girls in the special camp showed no differences in self concept from the non-handicapped girls who had attended the regular camp. Not only were their tests no different from the normal girls, but they showed almost the same pattern of differences from the integrated handicapped girls as did the normal girls.

Two differences, however, did emerge. The segregated handicapped significantly more often than the integrated handicapped girls said they were *Sick* and *Lonely.*

One might understand the segregated girls more often saying they were *Sick* if one assumes the children were referring to physical disability. The children in the special camps were, in fact, more severely disabled, although we had tried to choose among the less functionally disabled in selecting our sample to interview.

But it is not clear why the segregated girls more often said that they were *Lonely*. Among boys too, the handicapped boys in the segregated camps used the word *Lonely* more often. It is puzzling, since in fact, they had more extensive relationships with other campers than did the integrated children. One possible explanation is that the segregated children were more open about their feelings, more emotionally expressive, and were less likely to hide their feelings of loneliness away from home.

To summarize, the differences in self concept for girls seem highly related to social structure. The handicapped girls in the integrated camps reported generally more negative self concepts than did their normal campmates or the handicapped girls in the segregated camps. The latter group had no different self concept than non-handicapped girls.

Self Concept of Boys

The results with the boys are generally in the same direction as the girls, but more complicated.

In the integrated camp three adjectives distinguished the handicapped boys from their normal peers. They were more likely to say they were *Lonely* and *Slow,* while the non-handicapped boys more often said that they were *Fast:* differences in felt social competence and feelings of productiveness.

But the segregated handicapped boys, unlike the handicapped girls in their camp, who tested no differently than normal girls, did show more negative self concepts than normal campers. They were different in mood (more *Sad*), felt social competence (more *Lonely*) and felt productiveness (more *Weak, Sick,* and *Slow*).

There were also many differences between the two groups of handicapped boys. The segregated boys significantly more often said that they were *Weak* and *Sick*, but on the other hand, more often said they were *Fast, Angry,* and *Noisy.* They less often said that they were *Slow* or *Plain-looking,* compared to the integrated handicapped boys.

The segregated handicapped boys were, in fact, the most severely disabled in the study, and their more frequent choice of *Sick* and *Weak* may not be unrealistic if they are referring to their disability. Yet despite their recognition of their physical limitations, compared to the integrated handicapped boys they saw themselves as more productive and socially competent, and they were more emotionally expressive.

SUMMARY

That self concept is negatively affected by physical handicap is clear from our data. Only one of the four handicapped groups showed as positive a self concept as the non-handicapped children.

The segregated camp structure had a positive effect on self concept for both handicapped girls and boys. Despite the fact that they were at least as physically limited, the disabled children at the segregated camp felt more generally competent than the integrated handicapped children.

The results emphasize the strong effects of environment on children's self concepts. They make us painfully aware of the ephemeral quality of self reports in personality studies. Personality is a constant only if we ignore the setting in which the measurements are conducted. But we are left with the important question: to what extent will the descriptions of self concept which we obtained endure beyond the camp experience?

SELF CONCEPT AND SOCIAL STRUCTURE

Another question we are left with has to do with understanding the *process* by which social structure affects self concept. The links connecting the structure of the setting and the behavior of the individual have been alluded to frequently in this volume, but not always made explicit.

The social structure of the integrated camps imposed conditions which led to a lowering of self concept, while the segregated camps' conditions improved self concepts. One approach to understanding the process is from the point of view that the individual's evaluation of himself is derived from his comparison of himself with others. In integrated camps, with the more competitive orientation, the physically handicapped child, compared to the physically normal youngster is most often second best. In the segregated camp there is always someone worse off to compare with.

Another approach to understanding self esteem is in terms of the concept of competence (White, 1959) which emphasized the role of accomplishment in giving a person the feeling of self-worth. In the integrated camp, the handicapped child playing by normal rules had not too often a feeling of competence through accomplishment because his abilities may not have been suited to many of the camp's activities. These are designed for the more physically able, average person. Many times he may overcome the difficulties and succeed, which may be highly rewarding. At other times he may be aided by counselors or friends to reach an adequate level of performance, and again feel a sense of accomplishment. But there are many other instances in which he fails or is excluded because he is holding up the game.

In the segregated camp there may be more opportunities to taste success for any child because of the care given to adapting activities and rules of play to the participants.

Still a third way of thinking about the effect of social structure upon self concept is through the concept of anxiety. The essence of anxiety may be conceived as uncertainty (May, 1950). Where the situation in which the person is involved is an ambiguous and uncertain one; where he must take action yet cannot foretell the results of his action, that person will feel anxiety. For the physically handicapped child, the integrated camp often is an ambiguous situation where there is frequent uncertainty to him and to others, about his being able to participate at an acceptable level.

Compounding the uncertainty is the disinclination encouraged by the staff to openly face and talk about the handicapped child's special concerns and needs. They are treated "like everyone else". If the child's disability remains unnoticed and not discussed, the social or functional limitations it imposes on him remain unclear. He is never sure if he can make it or not when he engages in an activity unless he is highly experienced in that particular event. Probably this uncertainty contributes to the child's negative conception.

At the segregated camp, where the goal is not to compete against a standard, but to participate, the child is likely to feel more certain. He is more likely to feel he *can* perform because the game will be adapted to him.

But we know, of course, that the conditions of a social setting alone do not shape an individual's feelings about himself or herself. Much depends upon the match between the individuals' values and abilities and the particular social setting he finds himself in. This is illustrated in the case studies which follow, and is further discussed in the last chapter.

Chapter Twelve

ALEX AND NORMAN

FIVE youngsters out of 123 boys at Camp Cherokee had physical handicaps. Two were integrated into the oldest village unit. They were approximately the same age, had the same set of counselors and interacted with the same children each day. Their case studies are presented so that the social structure and its affects on their adjustment to camp can be discussed. They are not meant to show different personality characteristics.

The studies of Alex and Norman show that the adjustment each child made is in large part a reflection, not of the specific camp or individuals involved, but of the social structure and values inherent in the camp and cultural setting of the country.

At Camp Cherokee in the village for oldest campers (aged 13-16), Alex and Norman, Easter Seal campers, were among seventeen children living in two-man tents, cooking their own dinners and participating in scheduled activities.

Alex was a fifteen year old boy, post-polio, who wore braces, used crutches and was considered by campers and counselors alike to be well adjusted at camp.

Norman, aged fifteen, had cerebral palsy. He wore no braces, used no crutches, but had poor motor coordination and walked slowly. His speech was affected by his CP and he spoke slowly in an atonal voice. He was not considered a good camper by his village mates or counselors. His adjustment to the group was thought to be poor and counselors expressed their concern about his fitting into the regular program.

ALEX: "A WELL ADJUSTED CAMPER"

Social Background

Age: fifteen years

Family: One brother, 17; one sister, 10

Father's occupation: Policeman (photographer, electrician, carpenter in off-duty time)
Mother's occupation: Housewife

School: Attends neighborhood public school, 8th grade

On Campership sponsored by hometown civic organization which sends handicapped children to camp each year.

Medical Background

In 1955 when 18 months old, Alex contracted polio. He now has full right leg disability with partial left leg disability.

Alex wears leg brace (right leg) and uses crutches. According to Alex, brace costs $600.00 when new. He has had his present brace for six years and is expecting to get a new one when he returns home from camp. His present brace breaks about once a week and is usually fixed by his father who welds it together.

Alex's medical application shows him to be in excellent health with no dietetic restrictions, medications, or activity restrictions. He is said to have no special problems in terms of his emotional, mental or neurological development.

Physical Description

Alex is average height, has dark hair, and a pleasing, friendly manner. His shoulder and chest muscles are highly developed and seem in sharp contrast to his legs which are muscularly under-developed from lack of use. He uses full wooden crutches and moves with decisiveness and vigor. At the moment, Alex is walking back to his village from the swimming area and is talking animatedly to a friend.

From fieldnotes 7/13/69

The superior development of Alex's shoulder and chest muscles was one of the first characteristics mentioned when counselors were asked about his early adjustment to camp. A few days after camp started, it became clear that Alex had been lifting weights for years to help develop his chest and shoulders.

Alex's Early Adjustment to Camp

Counselor #1: Um, he fit in pretty fast, I'd say; faster than a lot of the others. Like his handicap is overlooked completely. Like he'll play games. The upper half of his body is really strong, you know. Like I saw him lifting weights the other day. I think he could beat everyone. You know, that really helped him, like positioning himself in the group.

Counselor #2: Alex? I think he is very normal. All the kids really like him. Just one or two things, like the dance. He was kind of sad last night because he couldn't dance with any of the girls. Sometimes he shows off a little bit with his muscles, but he's pretty normal and the kids like him.

Counselor #3: At the beginning, very quickly Alex found a friend and he helps the others too. And everybody feels that he is an amazing boy because he is able to build himself up so amazingly, you know. The other day he was lifting weights and he's incredible. I think he can lift. . . . On his back, he can lift about as much as Hugh [counselor and college football star who prides himself on his muscular development] , which is a feat. People talk about Alex with admiration.

From interviews 7/18/69 to 7/19/69

On the second day of camp, Alex was observed doing tricks by one of the fieldworkers:

The boys like to ask Alex about his terrific strength and arm muscles. At the moment while I am writing these notes, he is on the ground showing them tricks with his very weak "muscleless leg" (right leg). He can throw it up behind his neck and then turn over and walk on his hands. Or, he can throw it up behind his head and then get up on the crutches, and supporting himself on his arms, walk around.

From fieldnotes 7/13/69

Eight days later, these notes were recorded:

It seems that Alex is not only accepted but looked up to by many of the boys because of his great muscular development. He often challenges others to Indian wrestle with him while kneeling or when sitting at a table. He inevitably wins. And, he continues to amuse the boys with his acrobatics while making fun of his legs and crutches.

From fieldnotes 7/21/69

Alex continued to perform physical feats and when his village group was to leave camp for a three day overnight trip, he and all campers were given their choice as to whether they wanted to go on a long hike or short hike. The long hike was described as daily mountain climbing along different mountain trails. The short hike meant less walking and involved visiting various points of interest in the area. Alex signed up for the long hike; counselors assigned him to the short one.

Friends and Social Interaction

Campers were transported to The Mountains in a camp bus. As soon as the bus arrived at the camp grounds of the park and all the equipment was unloaded, the kids began setting up their camp. Alex was immediately joined by Will, the boy in the village who is quite obese. He asked if he could share the tent with Alex as he walked slowly with him behind the rest of the group from the bus to the field. The two seemed to be friends at the campsite and on through the rest of the day.

From fieldnotes 7/15/69

Alex's tentmate was Will, the obese camper from his village group. When interviewed, Alex later said that Will was his best friend. However, Alex joined other campers for most activities. As described in fieldnotes of July 15:

Alex is able to do most everything except walk quickly. He does a lot of things while sitting on the ground. And, at that he is superb. For example, setting up a tent he does beautifully because he just crawls around the tent or sits there and arranges things very nicely. Sitting at the table he is fine. He can play arm wrestling games and other things sitting down. He sits down more than the other kids do.

I noticed that Alex went on all the walks that the other kids assigned to the short hike did. Even on one walk which was almost a mile; he walked along with his crutches. It is possible for him to go short distances, for example to his tent, or to the picnic tables of our campsite (about 30 feet) without his crutches, bracing his right lower leg with his right hand.

From fieldnotes 7/15/69

The lake is cold and the raft is far out in the middle, but Alex went swimming with the others. Out on the raft, he pulled himself up onto the diving platform so that he was at the same eye level as the fellows who were standing around talking. When Alex swam back to shore and was coming out, two boys ran to get his crutches for him.

From fieldnotes 7/16/69

Alex's Acceptance by Some: Rejection by Others

By the end of the intense experience the boys shared on the camping trip, Alex was thought to be very much a part of the group. Back at Camp Cherokee, he went to all the activities his village mates did, although he did not always play with them. When interviewed, Alex said that he did not enjoy playing when he knew he would hold up the game. Non-handicapped children seemed to appreciate this point.

Interviewer: How about Alex? Does he slow things up?

Kenneth: [non-handicapped boy, 15 years old] : I don't think so; I think he actually quickens them up because he's really very competitive. If you see him, he doesn't want to give up on anything. And like he'll substitute his hands, you know and the top of his body for his legs, and he'll, ah, do quite a bit of things better than anybody else, I'd say.

But when he knows he can't do something well, then Alex doesn't get in the way of others. Like he was the one who wanted to be a referee in yesterday's baseball game and I think so that he wouldn't have to play.

He's worked on his physique, you know, and I think he's more of an asset than he is an injury to the group.

From interview 7/19/69

In his interview, Alex indicated his high value for athletic activities. Of all the things he liked to do, he enjoyed horseback riding and riflery best. He said that he was "pretty good" on horses compared to most kids his age and that he and his brothers used to train racing horses for his grandmother who owned a stable.

Interviewer: How about shooting? How are you at that?

Alex: I'm good. I can even outshoot my father and he's a policeman.

From interview 7/18/69

All campers did not accept Alex, however, as a group member. There were normal boys who felt negatively about Alex and Norman, primarily because of their having physical handicaps.

Weston [non-handicapped boy, 14 years old]: There are two abnormal kids; I mean there's one that's looney and another who is a cripple. Alex had polio when he was born and Norman is a little retarded, I think. The other kids in our village . . . I mean, they want nothing to do with Norman and Alex. I mean, they're really outcasts. They're in a different category completely.

Interviewer: They are?

Weston: Yeah, well one of them, Alex, the kid who had polio, he's out. He's not actually out of it. He's not actually out of the group completely because he still has his brain, you know. He can still think and talk with you and everything, discuss stuff with us.

Um, Norman is really not communicating with anybody; he really can't understand anything because he's not really capable of thinking things out. I think everybody knows that there isn't any communication between Norman and anybody else.

Interviewer: So you'd say that Alex is a little more in than out?

Weston: Oh yea, I mean he's in more with the group because he isn't that restricted. I mean his legs, he doesn't have his legs, but he's got everything else and he still can walk.

But Norman isn't very, very . . . I mean I don't enjoy talking with him. Um, I don't like to really see people like that. It isn't very. . . . I mean it doesn't make you feel good to see something like that and, I really wouldn't want to sleep with him . . . with either one of them, or anything like that.

From interview 7/19/69

Alex's humor was in large part disparaging remarks about being handicapped. He liked to laugh openly at his awkwardness and unusable leg. At one point in his camping session, he enlisted the help of his village mates in hiding his disability. The occasion was a dance with a nearby girls' camp.

Male Counselor # 1: Alex got to the dining room (dance hall) before the girls arrived. He sat down on a bench and putting one leg up, he told everyone to tell the girls if they asked that he'd broken his leg or he's sprained his ankle, or something, so that they wouldn't think he was that bad . . . that he had polio.

From interview 7/20/69

As one camper stated it, Alex can't do all the things we do but he can do enough so he's still one of the guys. Alex said that he felt liked.

Interviewer: Would you say that you are liked or not liked?

Alex: I'm liked (Why?) Because I don't pick fights a lot. Because I don't give them all the lip some of the other kids do.

From interview 7/18/69

Not only did Alex not like to pick fights, he hesitated to bother people even when his brace broke. One of the suggestions he had for improving the camp was to have his village group eat together in their village rather than eat some meals in the main dining hall. The suggestion can be seen as a reflection of his difficulty walking back and forth between his village and the main camp. Walking to the main camp dining hall meant walking along a long, rocky, hilly path with many exposed roots and large rocks.

Interviewer: Is there anything you could suggest to make camp better?

Alex: Having all the meals at the village instead of going down to the main dining hall all the time.

Interviewer: Why would that be better?

Alex: You don't have to walk so much.

Interviewer: Does it bother you to walk there?

Alex: Well, you see I broke my brace the other day and I can't use it. A couple of days before we went on that camping trip.

Interviewer: I see. What does that do for you, when you don't have your brace?

Alex: It just makes it a little harder, you know, for me to walk around. I can't walk as well.

Interviewer: Is there any way the brace can be fixed?

Alex: It has to be welded together. It has broken a lot of times before and my Dad has fixed it. It's not too hard to do.

Interviewer: Did you tell the counselors about it?

Alex: No, not yet. It doesn't bother me that much 'cause I get along fine without it.

Interviewer: Maybe if you showed them how to fix it they could get it welded for you.

Alex: I don't really mind. It doesn't slow me down that much except when we're playing baseball and I don't really want to play anyway. I'm not very good.

Interviewer: Why didn't you tell the counselors about it?

Alex: I didn't want to bother them about it.

Interviewer: You don't like to bother people about yourself?

Alex: No.

From interview 7/18/69

While he preferred to keep his handicap as unobstrusive as possible, not playing games when he would not do well, or not telling anyone about his broken brace, Alex still felt that his handicap made him different from other village members. All campers interviewed were asked if they were different or the same as the other children in their cabin.

Interviewer: You say you're different. In what ways would you say that you're different?

Alex: The others all act around the same, and they all get around better. I guess my handicap; that's about all.

Interviewer: How does that affect you?

Alex: I can't go very fast: I can go pretty fast but not that fast, doing jumps and stuff. Otherwise it doesn't affect me really, that much.

From interview 7/18/69

That Alex's excellent social adaptation is made at a high cost to his mood and his feelings about himself is revealed by his answers to the Like Me Test. Although the majority of the integrated handicapped boys described themselves as *Happy* (83%) and Smart (83%), Alex said those adjectives were not like him. Also he sorted *Lonely, Sad* and *Quiet* as like him whereas only one third or fewer of the Easter Seal children did likewise.

But, Alex ended his interview as follows:

Interviewer: Of all the people in camp, is there anybody that you would like to be like?

Alex: No, not really. I like being me.

From interview 7/18/69

Counselors and many campers indicated that they enjoyed having Alex part of their village group.

NORMAN: "A POORLY ADJUSTED CAMPER"

Social Background

Age: fifteen years
Family: One sister, 10

Father's occupation: Accountant
Mother's occupation: Housewife

School: Attends special, ungraded class

On Campership sponsored by Massachusetts Easter Seal Society

Medical Background

When seven years old (1961), Norman was in an automobile accident and suffered a traumatic blow to the head.

He has cerebral palsy resulting in right-sided spasticity and palsy. The handicap affects his balance, right foot and right hand coordination, and his fine motor movements.

Norman's speech is difficult, slow and atonal. He is slow in feeding himself, dressing and talking. Some but not all counselors felt he might be retarded.

Physical Description

Campers kept arriving today and within a few minutes after the gates opened, the place was swarming with boys, their families and relatives. The minute Norman arrived, I knew it was him. Without being told that a child with CP was in the group, an observer would immediately be able to see Norman as different from the others. Perhaps it is his stance, or the expression on his face.

His hair is blond, crewcut, and he is of average height and size. Two long scars go along the side of his face and head. He looks like a sad child. He stands in a poor posture and the look on his face is that of a child who is distant and out of it. His affect also seems unusual and when he spoke with others, Norman turned his head at a 90° angle so that one is left facing his ear. Perhaps he has some hearing loss also.

From fieldnotes 7/12/69

Norman's mannerisms were often found to be funny by his fellow campers.

It was raining today, torrential rains kept pouring down upon us. All camp activities were going to be held nonetheless, even swimming since there was no lightning or thunder. Norman shuffled down to the waterfront wearing a pair of cotton socks which were completely covered by mud. The rest of the boys were barefoot. Norman walks with a poor gait, dragging his feet rather than picking them up. His muddy socks caught the attention of some of the younger boys standing in line near the water. They started poking each other and whispering about the socks. When Norman was near to them, one said in a loud stage whisper, "I guess his mother told him to be sure and wear warm socks when it rains." (Laughter)

Because of his awkward manner, every act of his is looked upon negatively. He is not given the benefit of the doubt as someone more "normal" in appearance would receive. Norman might have been concerned about his athlete's foot condition.

From fieldnotes 7/13/69

Mental Ability and Early Adjustment

All of Norman's counselors considered him to be below the level of the other campers.

Counselor #1: I think the worst thing about him is that he just isn't mentally at our level; at least he doesn't seem to be. He seems very, very slow. He asks questions when it's already been explained. He doesn't do work that he should and he has to ask how to do everything. He leaves things around and constantly has to be told what he's going to be doing the next minute.

Counselor #2: I wonder if he'll ever fit in. He's a little uncoordinated and slow in speech. And I wonder how much he's aware of what's going on. Like if you tell him something, he'll understand, but he doesn't observe too much and is really dependent upon us.

Counselor # 3: I don't think the other kids will be able to play with him. I think Norman is in a mentally lower group, which could be expected, I guess. It's not his fault but some of the boys could never play with him, play ball with him; he doesn't seem with it at all.

From interviews 7/18/69 – 7/19/69

It was not clear, however, how much of Norman's slowness was a result of his poor speech. It was never clear whether Norman was actually retarded, thought to be retarded because he could not be understood and had awkward ways of doing things, or poorly motivated because of his communication problem.

Counselor # 2: He has a hard time, as I say, in speaking. He doesn't talk too much, that's one thing. Like, I don't know too much about him. Because no one really talks to him. Quite often you see groups of guys, you know, standing around in tents, but you never see him with them. He's alone pretty much, so that's one difference for him.

I guess his intellectual level is a little bit less than that of the other boys. But then, you know, no one *really knows him that well.* No one really notices him that much, so who knows the truth?

From interview 7/18/69

As recorded in fieldnotes:

Neil [head counselor for the village] began talking about his doubts concerning Norman. The main thing that bothered Neil was Norman's slow speech. It took a lot of time and patience to listen through to the end of what he had to say and usually what he had to say was not earthshaking.

From fieldnotes 7/10/69

Norman was often seen standing alone or sitting by himself, staring into space. Occasionally he made attempts to engage one or another of the campers into conversations, but often he was rebuffed by them as they hurried by. Early in his camp experience, Norman found that the details of his car accident were of interest to some of the boys and he used this as a way to get acquainted.

Norman set out from his village this morning saying that he was going to see if he could find someone to play tennis with him. He left with tennis racket in hand, looking for some of the younger campers from another village.

He was stopped by Hugh [counselor] who asked Norman why he had his tennis racket out when it was beginning to rain. Suddenly, seeing a boy he knew walk past, Norman grabbed Hugh's arm, shouting, "Tell him I got hit by a car."

Brandon [11 year old, normal boy] was a little taken aback by the fury of Norman's demand, and Hugh was surprised by the sudden change of topic. Hugh turned to Brandon and told him that Norman had been hit by a car. Brandon replied, "I believe you".

Hugh walked off and Norman asked Brandon to come with him to the lake and hit stones into the water. While they were taking turns throwing rocks, Brandon still interested in Norman's accident, asked him questions: "How did he get hit by the car?" "How old was he?" "Where was the accident?" Norman seemed happier than ever.

From fieldnotes 7/13/69

But perhaps as Counselor # 2 suggested, no one really noticed him or knew him well. Few children spent much time with Norman. On the camping trip to the mountains, some of the campers were asked directly to share a tent with him, but none agreed to do so. Norman made little effort to join the others either.

Norman is poor in almost everything he does and he doesn't attempt many things. For example, when it came time to set up tents, although none of the kids seemed to know how to do it, they tried by laying out the ground cloths, the tent halves, buttoning them together and trying to find stakes. Norman just sat on the ground looking around idly or dreaming. He didn't make an attempt.

The counselors tried to get one of the boys to share a tent with Norman but he refused. This was Jacob, who then set up his tent as a half tent, away from everyone else. Later he converted it to a full tent, but kept it to himself.

From fieldnotes 7/15/69

Although Norman's slowness was a result of his cerebral palsy, it was not clear as to how much he could do or how fast he could go. Some attributed his slowness to lack of motivation.

> Norman is slow walking and drags behind the others. He is always the last to finish meals. The others are done 15 minutes before he is. He is also the last on walks and and is often just left standing there by others. But, I noticed that when he feels in a good mood and wants to keep up with the others, he can do it. He can even run fairly fast. Yet, today he is isolated, socially and physically. Occasionally a fellow camper will stop long enough to say a few words to him, frequently in a patronizing way.

> From fieldnotes 7/16/69

Norman said that he wanted to be included in all the activities of the camp and expected to be part of the village teams or involved with all the others in activities.

> *Counselor # 1:* The difficult thing with Norman being part of the group is that he can do things, things that Alex can't do. I mean he can run; he can play baseball, but he sort of has to be the extra man on the team, because he does more harm than help. On the baseball team yesterday, we started off with even teams. Norman being on one team. But the side that Norman was on was behind 18 to 0 by the end of the four innings. It wasn't his fault, but the fellows had the feeling that they were one man short.

> From interview 7/18/69

Norman never voluntarily removed himself from any activities and it fell to the counselors to arrange a special role for him because teammates began objecting to his participation with them. With time, some of the normal boys did join the counselors in trying to help Norman find his place.

> *Counselor # 3:* The only thing that's true is that he doesn't fit in and you have to make exceptions for him. I think we all try to make exceptions for Norman. He probably won't do that much work at the village. Like he was supposed to help with dishes yesterday and he's not that much of a help. He keeps asking questions that are annoying.

> I think what we're going to have to do is try to get him into everything in a special way. It's very easy for us to just ignore him and

have him sit on the side of everything. In the working and everything, that would be easier but I don't think the campers would consider that either. We'll just have to keep working on the problem.

From interview 7/18/69

Reactions to Norman from his fellow group members were mixed. At times he was a source of amusement to the boys who made fun of him behind his back. At other times, campers and counselors tried to help him with various problems. The dance with the neighboring girls' camp shows the varied reactions to him. Campers began practicing their dancing a few days before the event.

> *Counselor # 2:* They had music in one of the tents and were showing each other different dance steps. Norman was in there and they had him standing up front trying some out. I eventually stopped that because some of the fellows were laughing out loud. Anyway they were supposed to go to bed. I felt that Norman was having a great time for awhile, but I thought maybe he'd catch on that they were laughing at him. But, he was funny. You should have seen him.

> Luckily it's a mature enough group so that they're not trying to hurt him; to make fun of him and have him know that they're making fun of him. When Norman started dancing, most of the guys thought that was funny but only a few laughed out loud and others thought that they should stop the whole thing themselves so that he wasn't made a fool of.

From interview 7/18/69

Everyone was concerned about Norman at the dance. Norman was concerned himself. When the evening was underway, he approached a village counselor to find out how one goes about asking a girl to dance. As his counselor stated it:

> *Counselor #1:* Everyone was really worried about that dance, what he'd do. And finally when he asked me I got him to go ask one of the girl counselors. That started it. He danced and no one bothered him very much. He was funny, if you really looked at him; he's uncoordinated because of his accident. But he did dance and he danced quite a few times. He asked some girl campers, too. But he can't associate with them. He can't talk to them. It was just one dance

and then leave. But still I think that's probably a step forward for him. I don't think he's done that before.

From interview 7/18/69

When asked if he thought he was liked, Norman said that he couldn't think of anyone who liked him; "Maybe," he said, "there was one camper who likes me." Norman could not recall the friend's name, but said that he wears a blue shirt sometimes and is from a younger village. Actually, only two campers mentioned Norman when listing their friends at Camp Cherokee. Alex was one; Walter was the other.

Walter at age four had been involved in a traffic accident which resulted in his having slight brain damage also. Walter was considered backward; he was a member of the next younger village group. Also rejected by many cabinmates, he noticed Norman during the early days of the camp session and stated that he was drawn to people like him.

Interviewer: Who are your friends at camp?

Walter: Do you remember Norman? He is in the oldest village and was on the camping trip, too. Well, he's a good friend of mine.

Interviewer: Norman? What's he like?

Walter: He's a good kid even though he does have a voice problem, but that doesn't matter to me. I mean even if . . . even if . . . . I have this friend who's mentally retarded and he's one of my very best friends at home. I really care for them kind of people. I mean, I really like them.

Interviewer: Why do you like them?

Walter: Because I can understand them. Like you know, I can have feelings for them, sort of. I just understand them.

Interviewer: Do you feel that you can understand Norman maybe better than the other guys can?

Walter: Yeah, he needs like a bodyguard, Norman does. When they bother him, I can say, "Get away; go away and leave us alone," when kids bother us too much.

From interview 7/16/69

Norman found Alex attractive as a friend because of his handicap and mentioned Alex as his only friend. The two were rarely observed together.

Interviewer: Who are your friends at camp?

Norman: Alex! (Why?) Because he. . . . 'Cuz he has something the matter with him, just like me.

Interviewer: Well, why do you like him?

Norman: I don't know. I just like him. Alex's handicapped. In a way, he's just like me.

From interview 7/19/69

Norman described himself as being slow:

"I'm slow at doing things, and my speech. . . . Speech is not good."

From interview 7/19/69

But most of the integrated handicapped boys thought they were slow. On the Like Me Test two thirds of that group sorted *slow* as like them. Norman did give a more negative picture of himself than most of the Easter Seal campers on the LMT. While most of them said they were *Strong* (67%) he did not. On the other hand he described himself as *Lonely* as did only one-third of the Easter Seal children.

Norman was not sure about how he felt on seven of the LMT adjectives, showing far more indecision than any other camper. He said he, "Didn't know" about the words, *Weak, Strong, Noisy, Quiet, Tired, Busy* and *Sad.*

It would be no unfair conclusion that Norman was confused about himself and uncertain about how he is perceived by others. Norman ended his interview by saying that he would like to be someone else.

Interviewer: If you could be anyone else in camp, who would you most like to be like?

Norman: Um (sigh, long pause), Um, Um, I would be like. . . . Does it have be just one person?

Interviewer: No.

Norman: Oh, I would like to be like the other boys, except not Alex. I would like to be like them because, um, they can do lots of stuff I can't.

From interview 7/19/69

DISCUSSION OF CASE STUDIES AT INTEGRATED CAMPS

Values and Social Structure

Camp Cherokee was a camp designed for normal boys. The emphasis was on an active athletic program, including overnight camping trips, and competitive sports. In the social structure where cabin and village groups were scheduled to play against one another and where there were Olympic events in which children raced against time and each other, competition was an important part of each day's social interaction. It is interesting to view the two cases in terms of these values and the values held by each handicapped child.

Alex, the "well-adjusted" camper, valued competition perhaps above all else. He worked on developing his chest and arm muscles so that he was superior to most of the non-handicapped children. He constantly reasserted this superiority by frequent challenges to the other campers to Indian wrestle or lift weights. His superiority in this respect was talked about frequently and Alex enjoyed performing physical feats whenever possible.

Alex shared a competitive spirit with other campers. He was careful not to participate in any activities he felt he could not perform well and, in so doing, he rarely held up the rest of his group. He participated in their winning or losing in a perfunctory way, (referee, time keeper) and did not ask them to include him on the team. It was not necessary for them to alter the game so he could play.

Fellow campers had to walk more slowly if they were walking with Alex to or from activities or dinner, but such a slowing down on the part of the non-disabled camper was minimal in the case of Alex.

Norman, "a poorly adjusted camper", on the other hand, did not hold the value of competition. His handicap was such that either he did not have the mental capacity to understand the point of view, or he was unwilling to withdraw when he would hinder the competitive process.

Norman expected to be included in all activities. He wanted to play baseball and it meant that his teammates had to change the game so that they could pitch a slower ball to him.

Because of his speech defect, others had to slow down to have a conversation with Norman. They had to alter their pace of listening, thinking and talking. It is interesting to compare Norman's adjustment in his group with that of another handicapped camper having a speech problem. Rebecca was a ten year old girl, born deaf. She actually had less speech than Norman. However, Rebecca was better accepted by her cabinmates than Norman. She was frequently asked to join the others who were talking and joking or going to activities.

There are several important differences between Rebecca and Norman. First, Rebecca almost always understood what was going on. If she did not read lips enough to hear the words, she was adept at catching on to the meaning of what others were doing. Second, Rebecca did not slow others down. Perhaps Rebecca's actually having less speech available to her than Norman had was an asset in the social structure and interaction in a camp setting. She made her own thoughts known with the use of hand motions, facial expressions and a few, well-chosen words. Norman had been trained to say whole sentences, to pronounce each word distinctly and well.

Norman's slow speech required others to stop and listen to him before his ideas could be understood. Rebecca did not slow others down, but rather conversed at their pace with her short-hand gestures. She was limited, however, in the complexity of the thoughts she could express and when others were involved in rap sessions, she often stayed by herself reading a book or engaged in another task. However, she was part of her cabin group while Norman's village-mates tended to pass him by. As one of his counselors stated it, "I don't know too much about him because no one really talks to him."

Inclusion of handicapped children into their peer groups can be seen in terms of the sharing of those values important in the various social structures and pacing of each. With the handicapped person, physically or mentally handicapped, group norms or sharing group values is not always a matter of choice. Goffman states it in this way:

> It can be assumed that a necessary condition for social life is the sharing of a single set of normative expectations by all participants, the norms being sustained in part because of being incorporated.
>
> Failure or success at maintaining such norms has a very direct effect on the psychological integrity of the individual. At the same time, mere desire to abide by the norm; mere good will is not enough, for in many cases the individual has no immediate control over his level of sustaining the norm.

(Goffman 1963, pp. 127-128)

Alex understood and shared the non-handicapped children's interests and values. He had the mental capacity to do so and could withdraw in those situations when he felt he would annoy or antagonize others. Alex had great disdain for his handicap. His humor involved making disparaging remarks about his awkwardness or his unused legs. He went so far as to lie about being handicapped when girls came to the camp for a dance. For acceptance, Alex fashioned himself after the normal standard and worked to meet that standard as closely as possible. He also developed his upper chest muscles so that he might actually participate in physical competition with others.

If a handicapped child cannot abide by the norms shared by the group, it is important to examine what this means to others. Each person's position in the group is affected by the performance of others.

The village of oldest campers at Camp Cherokee had no choice.

Norman and Alex were part of their group. Ignoring Norman was not altogether successful because it produced guilt feelings in the non-handicapped children. He was constantly present. Something had to be done with Norman; ignoring him did not make him disappear. Including him in the group had its consequences also. Counselors were constantly faced with the difficulty of meeting the specific needs of handicapped and normal campers at the same time. Keeping Norman involved required more energy than not having him integrated into the main activities. Norman's needs were sacrificed to those of the majority.

Because of the unclear nature of his handicap, some children blamed his differentness on his lack of trying or on his personality. Once the blame was removed from his handicap, it was possible to ignore him without the same accompanying guilt feelings, but normal youngsters still had to interact with him.

In the camp setting where competition was a part of the social structure, each child was concerned with his own performance. To be part of a winning team, each individual had to keep his performance up to par with those of his teammates. Although it has been suggested that handicapped children benefit from being on a winning team although their individual performance is poor, it appears that the handicapped children were well aware when their performances were inadequate.

Non-handicapped campers who felt sympathetic towards the handicapped youngsters, expressed the conflict they were in themselves. While they often wanted to help some of the handicapped players they felt that they could not do so without jeopardizing their own position with the group. They had to maintain a high enough level of performance to satisfy other team members.

The American value system stresses helping those less fortunate, but our own data suggests that non-handicapped children intent on their own position with their peer group did not respond to this value. This is in contrast to the segregated camp where helping and cooperation were the values stressed and it was possible for children to help without it interfering with their own needs of the moment. The children in the segregated camp did not strive to excell individually, therefore it was not necessary for them to be performing at their best at all times.

It is not surprising that such a camper as Alex who voluntarily removed himself from those situations in which others would have to slow down for him was accepted by others. Norman did not appreciate the competitive position of the normal children. He expected to be included at all activities and when he was not, he felt rejected time and time again.

What might have been the adjustment of Alex and Norman if they had been at Camp Woodland? Alex, a highly competitive person, would most likely have felt hampered by his values. He would have had to subordinate his physical prowess so that those less fortunate than he could participate. Again, he would not have been accepted fully for himself but only partially, in terms of his ability to go along with the requirements of the social structure. Norman, on the other hand, might have been more accepted, despite his constant need to be helped.

It is helpful to look at two female campers also approximately the same age and placed in the same cabin at Camp Hiawatha. Vickie was eleven years old, in a cabin with youngsters of 9 and 10 years. It was hoped that her slight retardation would be less a problem. She had difficulty in motor tasks although it was not clear to campers and counselors whether this was due to physical disability or problems in personality and motivation. By some campers, Vickie was not thought to be handicapped although there was general agreement that Vickie was odd.

During the winter, Vickie attended a special school where she was under less pressure to perform rapidly or at the same level that her chronological age mates were in regular schools. Her parents frequently praised her when she tried to accomplish tasks difficult for her and she was aware that she was slower than most children. She had been taught that she was not to judge herself by what others did, but rather was to feel pride for what accomplishment she was able to make

Vickie's cabinmates were concerned about how she made her bed. Each morning all the cabins were inspected by the camp nurse and points were awarded. During the entire camp session, Vickie's cabinmates were concerned with her performance and varied in their behavior between trying to make the bed for her (a fact which annoyed Vickie), or trying to ignore her (a fact which annoyed the non-handicapped children because they inevitably lost points).

When interviewed, many of the non-handicapped children stated that they found Vickie's insistence that she was doing well for "a person like me" more annoying than the fact that she could not make the bed well. The normal children objected to her lack of competitiveness or desire to work at it, or improve.

As in Norman's case, Vickie did not have competitive values or the mental ability to understand her annoyance to others so that she could withdraw in such circumstances as Alex could. Vickie, like Norman, stated that she would have preferred not being herself, but would have liked being like the other children, the normal children. She suffered from continual non-inclusion by her peers while Rebecca [congenital deafness], sharing the competitive drive, accepted other's conditional acceptance of her.

All but two of the campers with handicaps in Hiawatha and Cherokee preferred their camping placement over the possibility of attending a special camp. These children were competitive and striving despite their physical limitations. They preferred to be a part of a group of non-handicapped children and would have considered it a step backward to be segregated in a camp for handicapped youngsters.

At the integrated camp, the handicapped children were expected to be more self-sufficient and most strove to accomplish this. The desire to be integrated with non-handicapped children was best summed up by Norma, a 15 year old girl with cerebral palsy using braces and crutches.

> *Norma:* Um, a lot of people feel that, um, I should go to a camp that is for handicapped children, but I don't. I like the way this camp is run. I don't think there could be any better way of running a camp. In fact, I think that the special camps let the kids get away with too much; they do too much for you and the kids get too lazy. Here, even if you do have crutches, you still follow the same program and nobody caters to you.

> *Interviewer:* Um.

Norma: I like this. I like being independent, all by myself, having certain responsibilities to do.

From interview 7/5/69

Vickie [CP, retarded, motor involvement] said that she would have preferred a camp with a slower pace.

Interviewer: Well, would you rather be in a special camp?

Vickie: Yes, I don't like to do too much of the work. I don't mind helping or working a little bit. But there's too much work here.

Interviewer: Like what?

Vickie: Like they keep us too busy. I can't go that fast. We only have 15 minutes to do our cabin duties. I can't just take that long. I need some help. I'm slow.

From interview 7/6/69

In the segregated camp a few of the less disabled children stated that they would have preferred attending a regular camp where games were played, "as they are supposed to be played" and "not watered down."

The purpose of the case studies has been to show the relationship of "acceptance" of handicapped individuals in terms of their values and those shared by the group of which they are a member. Children like Norman and Vickie were not highly competitive. Perhaps they were not able to be so because of their mental capacities, or perhaps they had been taught by parents to judge themselves in terms of their assets and not in comparison with other children. (Dembo, Leviton and Wright 1956). They were often excluded from group participation. Not sensitive to the competitive concerns of their peers, they wanted to take an active part in sports and events despite others having to slow down to accommodate them. Including handicapped youngsters on teams with non-handicapped children changes the process of competitive play often to the deteriment of the normal player for the benefit of the slower one.

Alex, although physically limited, did not slow others down. The fact that he removed himself from the game released the non-handicapped youngsters and staff from guilt feelings produced by having to ask a handicapped person not to participate. Alex was happy at the integrated camp.

Chapter Thirteen

cccccccccccccccccccccccccccccccccccccccccccccccccccccccccc

JOAN

cccccccccccccccccccccccccccccccccccccccccccccccccccccccccc

CHILDREN who liked Camp Woodland returned year after year; those who did not like it, did not come back. Joan was one camper who was looked up to and admired by others. She had been the recipient of an honor camper award in past years. Joan loved Camp Woodland and was attending for her fourth summer.

JOAN: "A WELL ADJUSTED CAMPER"

Social Background

Age: Fifteen years
Family: Two sisters, aged 13 and 10

Father's occupation: Store manager
Mother's occupation: Community organizer for State Government

Education: Attends a private residential girls' high school. Transfered two years ago from a public school.

Medical Background

Joan has spina bifida, resulting in curvature of the spine and difficulty walking. Due to a chronic infection of her foot, Joan was not walking last summer. This summer she is walking, although with difficulty. Her gait is slow and poor.

She wears a half leg brace and uses crutches.

Physical Description

Joan appears to be a very likeable girl on first meeting; the type one is drawn to immediately. Perhaps it is her friendliness without aggressiveness or defensiveness. Perhaps it is a quality she exudes of having come to grips with her disability. She seems comfortable with herself, a quality which tends to make one who is talking to her feel comfortable also.

Joan is short, stocky, with overdeveloped shoulders. Actually, she looks like a box; a square from her neck down with short, protruding arms and legs. She walks slowly with crutches; bent forward. Her thighs are pushed together while her legs move below her knees, giving the impression that she waddles.

From fieldnotes 6/24/70

Meaning of Camp Woodland to Joan

To Joan the most important thing about camp seemed to be that it was restricted to disabled children, enabling her and others to learn to accept themselves as *different* yet *not alone* or unworthy. The camp gave her a feeling of group identification which she felt was a crucial first step for understanding oneself. In her interview, she expressed it this way:

Interviewer: How do you feel about coming to camp?

Joan: I look forward to it you know. I like it a lot. I think being with the kids we learn a lot about each other and correct each other. Say someone in school had a problem, they might have a hard time with the normal kids, or some of the kids would laugh at them. This happens quite a bit.

Well, until a person can learn to really accept the fact that he or she is handicapped, you know, the fact that they are different, I mean rather *we* are different, you can't really get to know each other or ourselves.

Interviewer: How do you learn it?

Joan: I think it's easier to learn in a group like this. I have some very close friends here and I can talk to them. I don't know about anyone else but I can really express my feelings here. I think it is different in school because a lot of your problems are with the other kids.

From interview 7/16/70

While developing a positive self concept was the most important benefit from being segregated with other handicapped children to Joan, she also appreciated the opportunity camp provided to participate in various camp activities. Camp seemed to provide her with a chance to perform without competing, although sometimes she had to perform at less than her actual ability. Joan's acceptance of her own limited ability and identity with others like herself can be seen in this statement:

Joan: Like when we're playing kickball in athletics. I'm slow, too, you know. I'm not the fastest person in the world, but I don't mind slowing myself down at all really. I really don't. It's good that the kids, . . . that everyone can get involved in the game.

Like there was a time when I wasn't walking and gradually I just began to walk again and now I'm thankful anyway that I can do as much as I can. I realize what these kids are going through because they're so slow and I was so slow. So I don't mind slowing myself down a little for someone else's benefit.

From interview 7/16/70

Joan and her friends seemed well aware of the need for their help by youngsters less able than they. They voluntarily gave it. When the athletic director arranged two games of shuffle board for the older girls, Joan and a group of cabinmates decided that the teams were unfairly balanced and volunteered to shore up the weaker team. Their behavior was tied to the value of cooperation. To these girls the object of the game was not to win but to play and help others to play.

Cooperation and Competition

In general, Joan appreciated the opportunity to relax without having to compete:

Interviewer: You mentioned a special atmosphere here. What is it?

Joan: I think that it's because it's so relaxed. Everyone can enjoy themselves, yet still work on improving, you know, their disability. Everybody can really work together. I use the word "work" again.

Interviewer: What do you mean by it?

Joan: Well, we can work together. We can do all things together. Like when we went on our overnight hike this week, no one had to be assigned any specific jobs, like setting up tents or something. We just all went in and pitched in. One kid took care of the food while someone else helped with the tents. You know, you just do as a group, do things together and help out when needed.

From interview 7/16/70

Interaction With Others

Throughout her interview, Joan referred to the difference in tension she experienced when with children with handicaps or those without any disability. Joan felt comfortable and accepted, part of a group at Camp Woodland. She was, in turn, one of the most admired campers there. When asked whom they admired most, some counselors answered as follows:

Counselor # 1: I think Joan would be the one I admire most. She's gone through quite a bit and done a lot of things for herself. She's very talented for what she's been through.

Counselor # 2: I admire Joan most. She's come a long way. She can walk, and she had to force herself to walk. She wasn't walking last year because she had her toe amputated since she was two years old, and it hasn't healed right yet. She's in a lot of pain, I think, yet she's always cheeful and doing things.

Counselor # 3: Joan! She has a lot of problems herself, yet she's the one kids go to when they have problems. She's writing articles about being handicapped too. So far she has had one or two published in a state magazine.

From interviews 7/15/70

Describing herself in the Like Me Test, Joan's choice of

adjectives was highly representative of the average handicapped girl at Woodland Camp. She said she was *Happy* and *Noisy; Friendly,* and *Plain-looking; Strong, Smart, Healthy* and *Busy.* The only difference she showed from the rest of her group was in saying she was *Slow* rather than *Fast.* She sees herself positively, and realistically, no differently from her peer group or the group of non-handicapped girls at the integrated camp.

Joan was admired for her accomplishments in the face of her handicaps. At the segregated camp, focus was upon what each child *could do.* If a child spoke, even with difficulty, speaking was seen as a positive identifying quality. In the integrated situation when mixed with normal children, what a child *could not do* became the identifying quality. At the integrated camps, children were periodically reminded that some campers had physical handicaps but this tended to make the normal children feel guilty and resentful. In the integrated situation everyone's ability was measured against an idealized norm.

In the segregated situation, a child's ability was measured against a lesser standard, either the child's prior level of performance or the performance of the least capable member in the community. This in turn resulted in a more positive attitude toward physical handicaps.

Campers at the segregated camp talked about their handicaps upon occasion, joked about them. The following excerpt shows how a girl's disability becomes a means of identification and subject to jest:

> The girls in Cabin One were divided into three groups. Ben [dramatics staff member] explained that group members were to act out short skits about camp life. Others were to guess what was being acted out.

> When Joan got up, she did an imitation of Betty [counselor] saying, "This is a certain counselor when she goes home." Joan leaned down towards the ground and started gobbling up large quantities of imaginary food. Then she said, "This is the same counselor at camp." Lying down, Joan imitated a tired counselor and then one complaining about going on a diet. Betty guessed it was her almost immediately and was rolling on the ground laughing.

> Betty then stood up to do the next skit, saying, "Okay, I have an

imitation of a camper." She stood up, pressed her thighs together and with knees held motionless started waddling on her lower legs. It was obviously Joan. While waddling in this way, Betty shouted, "Okay, everyone! It's rest hour. I want quiet." The entire group laughed long and loud at Betty's skit. Loudest of all, from the minute Betty stood up and hunched over to walk, was Joan.

From fieldnotes 7/14/70

There were other examples of open discussion concerning her handicap between Joan and her friends, many of a more serious nature. This group of older girls talked about marriage, bearing children, and the possibility of committing suicide. Joan's overall view of Camp Woodland as a place where she and other handicapped children could talk and work together to "find oneself" was best summed up in the following statement:

The first day you arrive here everyone is happier. We all have had experiences which are similar; being at camp, the atmosphere at home, you know, being with other kids that aren't like us in a way. It sounds awful the way I'm putting it, but that's the only way I can express it. I think that mostly it's the fact that we're together and no one is really shy. You know we can all talk and things like that.

I think it's good. I know the kids at camp and I talk about being handicapped quite a bit, 'cuz I think it's good to get it out in the open and hear and compare experiences and surgeries.

Like there's one girl in our cabin who wears a brace and hates it. She really does; she'll talk about it with disgust.

We all get into moods like that, of course, and you just want to say, "Gee, if I could only. . . ." But with most of us it goes quickly and it comes quickly, so you hardly notice it. With Elinor, it stays quite a bit.

I probably noticed it because I wear a brace too. I would rather keep it than just shoes because I think I'm getting a lot of good out of it.

From interview 7/16/70

Interviews with other campers at the segregated camp reflected a positive feeling toward being segregated for the opportunity it provided to identify with others and participate in all activities. This was especially true for girls for whom performing well in physical sports was not as important. A very small number of boys did mention that they disliked playing in games where rules were altered or special equipment was substituted. Larry [legally blind] was one camper who resented watered down sports.

Interviewer: Would you like to be in a regular camp, then?

Larry: I think I would. I think I'd rather be in a regular camp because you have real baseball games instead of just running around. And, you can go horseback riding. You can do anything. You can go swimming without having to go in a separate pool. You can go out in a canoe without a life jacket. Well, you'd have to go out in a life jacket if you didn't know how to swim, but if you could swim, they wouldn't give you a life jacket.

And, you could do mostly all this stuff for yourself instead of having someone else do it for you.

From interview 7/13/70

The above statement was made by a youngster who valued competition and the challenge of stretching to do things beyond his ability. However, this was a minority statement. To all but a few, being segregated voluntarily was looked upon positively. The segregated social structure provided the opportunity to talk with others, participate together and experience a group identity.

Millie [CP, crutches]: I like it here because you get to do everything and I am always on the go. And, I like it because I see friends with my own problems and it's easier to cope with mine. I can see I am making it and you see how much better you are than some of the other kids. It's fun because you are having fun with other kids who have the same problems that you have.

Elizabeth [legally blind]: At home I don't have as much fun as here. The kids at home sometimes when we're playing ball, they don't ask me to play; they just keep on playing. Here, I can play everything.

Jim [CP, crutches]: (What do you like about camp?) Swimming, the counselors, the overnights, and um, you can have more friends here at camp than any other place. Like Pete . . . he and I get together and talk alot about things. I do things for him and he does things for me.

From interviews 7/13/70 — 7/17/70

Since being segregated was seen so positively, does it follow that the children studied in this camp situation had a different set of values than those observed in the integrated camp? Does it follow that Joan and the others would have enjoyed being segregated all the time? Not at all. Joan, as well as others who attended regular schools, stated that she wanted to be integrated with normal children. Twelve of the girls (70%) were integrated in regular classes at school while six boys (32%) attended regular classes.*

After expressing her happiness with the segregated camp, Joan was asked about how she felt being integrated for school.

Interviewer: Do you like going to a regular school then?

Joan: I like it a lot. I've had private tutoring with the other kids in the hospital and things like that, and I have felt that I'd rather be with kids that are physically normal than be with kids that are like me.

From interview 7/16/70

Another camper who felt positive about segregation stated her preference for an integrated school situation:

Interviewer: Do you prefer that [integrated school] to a special school?

Ruth: [arrested cancer, leg amputation] : I go to a regular school and I like it where I am because it's more of a challenge, you know, to keep up with the other kids and try to do what they do and try to get along with them. It's really a challenge.

Interviewer: Would you like to go to a regular camp, then?

Ruth: No, I like it here better. You know it's all year I have to push myself to sort of keep even or keep up with the kids, not only in school work. I mean I can do pretty well, but in activities . . . When I come for the summer, I don't want to have to push myself so I really

---

*It should be noted that six boys (32%) in this sample had vision problems and attended special schools where braille was taught.

have to keep up with the kids. You know with these kids they go about the same pace as I.

Like in activities, you know, we walk from school to a baseball game or something like that. Most of the kids will be very good about it; they'll wait for me, you know, (laugh). Some of them plow right on. I suppose they don't realize it, but I got used to it.

From interview 7/17/70

Another camper reflects the same attitude, preference for segregation in camp; integration in school.

Interviewer: Then why would you rather come to a camp like this than attend a regular camp?

Jayne: [CP, slight involvement] : I mean this is the only camp that I've ever come to. I don't really know, but I think if I were at a regular camp and I was swimming like, I'd be afraid that some of the kids wouldn't like the way I swim and they'd start off and look at me funny; something like that.

Interviewer: Do you worry about things like that during the winter at school?

Jayne: There is a certain boy who makes fun of me all the time. He'll call me names. I feel kinda funny because he's always got wise remarks to make. He used to be in all my classes but he's not now.

Interviewer: Would you rather go to a special school with other handicapped children?

Jayne: No, I wouldn't like that at all. I've always gone to public school and I'd rather go there.

From interview 7/14/70

Boys also expressed this preference for a segregated camp and integrated school.

Interviewer: How would you like to go to a regular camp?

Frank: [CP, slight motor involvement] : Well, I don't know. A regular camp? I really wouldn't care for it. I've been in this camp for five or six years now and I've been helping people and like it. If I were in a regular camp, I wouldn't be helping people and, I don't know, it would be harder to work in. There would be more tension than here.

Interviewer: Do you like going to a regular school?

Frank: Yes, I don't do too good on grades, but I wouldn't want to change.

From interview 7/21/70

The data suggests that the handicapped youngsters studied in Camp Woodland had the same values of competition, and responded to an integrated social structure as the other handicapped children did. However, they preferred one type of social structure for their camping experience; the other for intellectual development.

According to cognitive dissonance theory, it is not surprising that those children interviewed who experienced both integration and segregation stated that they preferred things the way they existed. On the other hand, since successful integration depends upon the fit between the deviant's abilities and disabilities and the group tasks, it also follows that physically handicapped children would prefer being segregated when in a camp situation where physical activities are paramount and integrated when in a school situation where intellectual and social skills are important.

The children at Camp Woodland saw themselves as limited in physical activities and seemed content to be in a situation where competition was avoided in that area of functioning. On the other hand, they did not consider themselves limited in the area of intellectual functioning and would have disliked the avoidance of competition in that area.

The point helps clarify Joan's further statement about being sexually segregated. While integrated with normal children, she attended a girls' school. She is a cheerleader since, "We don't play with boys." When she was in a coeducational public school she withdrew from competition in an area she felt limited and unsure of herself.

Joan: It's different at the school I now attend. Before I went to a co-ed high school and it was harder to accept, you know, that I am okay. Like other girls would go out for the girls' basketball team, and I can do it, but I mean, I wouldn't have tried out for the team there. At the private school where I go now, I am a cheerleader. We don't play with boys so it doesn't really matter. The girls just compete amongst themselves.

From interview 7/16/70

SUMMARY, COMPARISON AND DISCUSSION OF CASE STUDIES

These case studies compared campers' liking of their camps and their adjustment in relation to the values of competition and cooperation. Alex was accepted by his peers at the integrated camp for he valued competition as much as they did. He challenged others to Indian wrestle and remained champion in this activity. According to his counselors, "That really helped him; positioned him in the group." Although physically capable in many aspects, when his handicap did prevent him from performing well, Alex withdrew from the game. He did not like holding others up and in this way he did not require normal children to slow themselves down to accommodate him.

Norman, because of his intellectual capacity, or Norma because of her different interest from peers at her camp, did not hold themselves back from competitive situations and expected to be included in all activities. This meant that friends had to alter performances to accommodate them.

Although many times an outsider in the integrated group, Norma preferred being at an integrated camp where she was treated as if normal. She responded positively to the expectation inherent in the social structure that she could do what other children could do. Segregation was seen by her as relinquishing the responsibility for herself to others who "did too much for you."

Joan, at Camp Woodland, reacted positively to the lack of high expectations in terms of physical performance. She enjoyed the opportunity Camp Woodland provided for her to participate in all activities, whatever her ability, and to share her feelings and experiences as a handicapped person. In an area where she felt limited, camping, Joan preferred a release from the competition she sought in school.

Chapter Fourteen

A CHANCE TO CHOOSE

W E have been discussing handicapped campers and their normal peers. Actually the term normal is deceptive. As used in our American society, it is often confused with perfection or an *ideal* standard. Normal is used as a goal toward which people should strive. "One must act normal", implying that individual differences from the usual, common or ideal are abnormal. In the range of human variation, the ideal state labeled normal is actually only a small part of reality, but to save face, people in our culture cover emotional feelings and keep from revealing problems or thoughts to others for fear that they will not be considered normal. This pressure to conform to an American idealized standard, called normal, can result in many individuals feeling deviant. Acceptable human behavior is circumscribed by this standard of measure.

Both the integrated and segregated camps strove to make the handicapped child feel normal. There were, however, varying definitions of what being normal involved. The handicapped children were actually required to:

1. *Look normal* (surface appearance counted. Management techniques used to cover deviations).

2. *Perform normally* (performances were to be within tolerable time limits and style).

3. *Achieve normally* (end results were to be within acceptable standards or they evoked pity, tolerance).

4. *Participate in normal activities* (take part in activities deemed right and good for growing children).

173

The integrated social structure stressed looking normal, performing normally, and achieving normally over the need to participate. Unless a child could perform normally, he was excluded (expected to withdraw) from participation. This exclusion of different performers was accompanied by a narrow definition of most activities. An activity was defined in terms of its core properties, the traditional manner of play. *Para* characteristics were not considered part of the activity or valued positions. Marching was walking in time to music. Baseball was playing ball, not including umpire or other positions.

Looking normal at the expense of managing to keep oneself hidden from others is not the same as feeling like a normal person. Management techniques may provide social acceptance, but at the same time they may militate against honest relationships. Performing normally at the cost of withdrawing from all activities in which different ways of functioning will be obvious may actually create a feeling of disunity within the performer; he is not being truly himself. It is also questionable as to how "normal" a youngster feels participating in a watered-down sport.

In the segregated social structure, there was a release from having to appear normal, perform or achieve normally. It was felt by those committed to segregation that merely by participating in activities the American culture deems normal and right, the physically handicapped youngster would feel normal. Even if activities were altered to accommodate the children and resembled valued activities in name only, the assumption was that they would bestow a *feeling* of normalcy. By participating in such activities as camp craft, nature study, and "nightclubs", one can feel as if he or she is a worthwhile member of society, it was assumed.

All children in each camp were treated equally, but within the confines of the programs which emulated normal activities. There was little room to have the initiative for behavior come from the children; each camp pushed to help children reach and fulfill the expectations of the social structure which, in turn, reflected our society's expectations.

AGGRESSIVENESS AND SELF-ASSERTION
AMONG HANDICAPPED CAMPERS

We were interested in learning how the handicapped children dealt with the fact of their handicap in social interaction with others. It was striking to observe how gaining acceptance into the group, managing to approximate normalcy and waiting for clues from others overshadowed attempts to reveal oneself fully. Handicapped campers in the integrated camps shrank from making any definite statements about themselves or how they actually managed given their disability. A handicapped camper did not state publicly, "Here I am. This is what I can do and this is what I cannot do." "Here is my prosthesis and here is how I use it."

In other words, handicapped campers did not reveal themselves spontaneously so that others could learn about their limitations and help them make adjustments that might be suitable to both the handicapped and non-handicapped participants.

It has been suggested that one of the gains from integrating handicapped youngsters with normal children is that the latter will learn more about disabilities and develop tolerance through exposure. It was found, however, that non-handicapped children actually had little opportunity to learn about physical handicaps. The knowledge they did gain was based on speculation with friends when handicapped children were not present or furtive glances made when nobody was looking.

In the integrated camps there was a small number of normal children aggressive enough to initiate direct contact, asking questions of the disabled youngsters, thus giving everyone a chance to deal openly with the disability. The handicapped campers seemed to welcome this advance, although such aggressiveness was considered wrong by the staff and campers alike. The behavior was sometimes stopped by counselors and campers and the children were for the most part "mature enough so that they are not going to hurt anyone" by asking questions.

Staring was not considered an attempt on the part of the uninformed to satisfy their curiosity; it was interpreted as aggressive behavior, and ill mannered.

At the segregated camp there was evidence that some campers could accept themselves as they were and through this self attitude and self assertion, help others accept them. Perhaps, as Joan, the well-adjusted camper in the segregated camp indicated, being segregated helped one come to grips with their differences. However, there is no evidence in this research to indicate that such self-confidence and self-assertiveness can be comfortably carried into an integrated situation where the demands of the social structure are different. It would be worthwhile to study the same children in both types of social structures in the future.

EFFECTS OF SOCIAL STRUCTURE ON
SOCIAL RELATIONSHIPS AND SELF CONCEPT

Challenging these attempts to make handicapped campers feel normal is not to suggest that handicapped individuals should not participate in activities designed for the non-disabled person. Children observed for this study obviously enjoyed their camp experiences and gained from them. It is likely that some handicapped children did feel worthwhile because they were able to participate in valued activities, perhaps for the first time.

What is clear is that the social interaction between children attending the different camps did vary according to the social structure, and that there were accompanying differences in self concept. The effects of social structure on social interaction, social relationships and self concept could be conceived as in Table XI, reading down for the effects within a social structure and across at any level to compare between social structures.

If this line of interpretation and conclusion is correct, we see different social effects from the two social structures. Both have positive and negative attributes when judged by American standards. From the point of view of an individual's psychic comfort and feeling of ease, the segregated structure may be preferable because there are comfortable, supportive, open relationships among individuals and an acceptance of wide differences in human attributes and functioning. From the point of view of a society which values self-advancement and individual

TABLE XI

EFFECTS OF SOCIAL STRUCTURE ON SOCIAL RELATIONSHIPS
AND SELF CONCEPT

The Integrated Social Structure	*The Segregated Social Structure*
1. Stress on being normal results in denial-avoidance of differentness. Handicapped children are more defensive and concealing about themselves.	1. More open acceptance of differentness. Less defensiveness about physical appearance and style of performance.
2. Social interactions are less intense; the children do not get to know each other well.	2. Relationships are more direct and honest, dealing openly with problems related to physical limitations and reactions to them.
3. Less appreciation of others as personalities. More emphasis on accomplishments. There is greater motivation to produce, to compete and to win. Competing and winning become bases for acceptance by peers.	3. More interest in individuals as personal-social beings rather than as performers or producers. But motivation to be accepted as a person may reduce pace of participation or productivity.
4. Resulting interpersonal relationships are less emotional and more fluid. Continual uncertainty results in anxiety and less positive self concept. Individuals are more independent of others, more motivated and may be more productive.	4. Interpersonal relationships are closer, more emotionally expressive. Lower felt anxiety and higher self esteem; a greater feeling of certainty and competence. There is more helping and dependency on others.

achievement, the integrated structure may be preferable because it stimulates competition, independence and productiveness.

PLACEMENT OF INDIVIDUAL CHILDREN IN INTEGRATED OR SEGREGATED SOCIAL STRUCTURES

When faced with the choice of placing a specific child in a specific type of camp, several aspects should be considered: the individual's personal characteristics, values and needs at the time in his or her life, as well as the demands and expectations of each social structure. Some of the important issues are the child's values, typical pacing in activities, social skills, motivation, and emotional strength to tolerate the tensions of integration.

Values of the Child

The integrated camp stressed competition while the segregated camp emphasized cooperation. A good adjustment in each social structure for the individual depended in part upon whether the child personally held the same values as implied by the social structure. Within the integrated camp, handicapped children who valued competitiveness and independence made an adequate adjustment. Within the segregated camp, children who wished to excell personally were mismatched to this type of social structure. Good adjustment, then, is associated with the degree of fit between the values inherent in the social structure and those held by the individual participants.

Pacing

Rather than just how one performed, a crucial factor in group adjustment was the pace at which one performed. Those with a fast pace often refused to slow down to accommodate those slower or resented it when asked to do so. On the other hand, those with a slower pace were unable to keep up with others. In the integrated camps, when the discrepancy between personal pacing in speech, mental functioning, or physical ability was great, the result was an irritation between the individuals interacting.

The importance of this issue was observed repeatedly. A child who was born deaf and had little speech available to her was better accepted by her peers than a boy who could speak full sentences after years of speech therapy. The former, through the use of hand motions and facial expressions or one-word statements, could make her meaning clear without requiring the listener to slow down physically or mentally.

In physical activities, children with physical handicaps who wanted to do things by themselves but who needed more time were either helped by others to finish faster, or left behind while others moved on. At other times, they once again required the non-disabled youngsters to wait while they finished. Irriation could easily be caused when social interaction involved those with different pacing.

Personal Motivation

Some of the handicapped children observed in the integrated

camps thrived under the expectation of the social structure that they *could* perform as well as the other children. They were motivated by the implied challenge this presented to them. They worked toward meeting the expectations and were not overly frustrated when they did not actually perform as well as some others. They could recoup their energies time and time again and continue to perform at the best of their ability. These youngsters were highly motivated to produce in a competitive structure and on an individual basis.

Other children did not have this high motivation and were left frustrated and angry when their performance fell short of the desired level or when they were excluded from activities because they were limited. The expectation that they could perform "if they tried" did not serve as a motivational force but rather as a cause for feeling defeated.

Children who might have been frustrated if they could not fulfill the high expectations of an integrated structure seemed more able to perform at the best of their ability in a segregated setting when they were not striving to keep up with faster-paced youngsters. They had the room to experiment and perform in their own way, at their own speed.

It is not clear at this point if the less competitive child, after an experience of acceptance in a segregated camp, would be able to enter an integrated setting successfully. Nor is it clear that children should necessarily be placed repeatedly where they feel more comfortable. We do know that many of the segregated campers lived integrated lives with peers in normal schools and within the family during winter months and welcomed the variation provided by the special camp in the summer. These same children said that they wanted to remain in a regular school during the winter. Probably many handicapped children would best be served by both opportunities being available to them, switching from one structure to another.

USES OF SEGREGATION

Segregation is an emotionally loaded term for its long association with forced segregation of Blacks. It has been seen as the antithesis of the American ideal of integrating minority members into the melting pot America was aiming to be. But rather than forced segregation, the term as used here refers to voluntary forming of a community of fellow experiencers.

This definition can be applied to any group of individuals who get together because of some personal or social attribute which makes them feel deviant or different from the large community and in need of support or direction from people who share the same attribute.

In other words, we are talking about the benefits of segregation to such groups as the aged, women, Blacks, or the physically handicapped in American society. Grouping together can be seen as an effort to come to grips with personal characteristics one feels uncomfortable with because of a misfit with the social structure or discomfort with role expectations.

When grouping together with others "in the same boat" a person can learn how to deal with this characteristic. He or she can also gain new perspectives such as taking pride in being able to function despite having the social handicap of deviance from the majority or normal standard. Contrast the new perspective with the more commonly practiced view of seeing differentness in terms of its limitations.

In a segregated setting, it is possible to individually break out of society's roles. In time, with group support and power through organization, the large society may change.

As the women's movement grows in strength in this country, one can see an excellent example of how forming a community of fellow experiencers helps individuals reassess themselves and gain confidence. Women meeting with other women share their inner feelings about being in a male-oriented society and are showing evidence of productiveness left undeveloped previously when women attempted to fulfill the expectations of the society.

Blacks are members of another deviant group in American society which has recently gained from self-segregation. The whole change in our value system towards the acceptance of "black is beautiful" is a direct outgrowth of segregation in terms of individuals of like characteristics grouping together, gaining a redefinition of themselves and breaking with tradition and role expectations forced on them by others who do not share their same characteristics.

Besides the psychological gains to be gotten from participation in a segregated group, there are many practical gains from political power, lobby pressure, voter support and economic strengths which can follow voluntary segregation.

LIMITATIONS OF SEGREGATION

With a slight turn of the head, however, the limitations of segregation without accompanying integration can be seen. A person may become overly dependent on the segregated social organization which may be geared to meet his needs. He may lose the motivation to be a productive individual because the special grouping presents fewer problems, hurdles or challenges which require his stretching to adjust. It is adjusted to him.

One must be cautioned when thinking through the consequences and benefits of segregation to avoid confusing segregation with separateness. The emphasis in this study is the benefits of both types of social structure, especially the need to establish an optimum balance between them for the benefit of the individual. As segregation may benefit an individual at different times in his or her life between times of integration, so too an individual may benefit from being part of a cooperative and competitive social order.

COMPETITION AND COOPERATION

Competition and cooperation are fostered by the expectations of the social structure, programming and attitudes inherent in the organization hierarchy.

In the segregated camp, cooperation was most obvious. Although children placed in this type of camp also held competitive values, they operated cooperatively while at camp. There appeared to be a minimum of competition among cabin members and the camp group as a whole. In other words, there was little inter- or intra-cabin competition. Games were played for the enjoyment of all rather than to ascertain who performed best.

Only by inference could competition be said to be present. For example, children who restrained themselves from playing at their best level in order to cooperate with the group could simultaneously pride themselves at being physically more competent than those they were slowing down to accommodate. Thus some individual competitive values may have been gratified while group functioning overtly proceeded on a cooperative basis. There was pride in being able to cooperate.

It should also be remembered that many of the youngsters able to cooperate so easily in the camp setting, reported enjoying the competitive structure of their integrated schooling. Camps are physically oriented, a place where physical prowess is rewarded. The children in the study had physical handicaps. Perhaps this reflects a willingness to suspend competition in an area where the likelihood of winning is low.

In the integrated camps, competition was prevalent between individuals and between groups. But cooperation was observed, especially within cabin subgroups. Much of the camp lore was perpetuated to solidify cabin groups by reaffirming rivalry between them. "Cabin Six is better than Cabin Five" goes the camp cheer. "We are the Bears who will beat you true and fair!" Thus cooperation was established to serve the competitive motive existing between cabin groups.

Muzafer Sherif (1961) in the Robber's Cave Experiment illustrated graphically how ingroup cooperation is strengthened in direct proportion to the degree of intergroup hostility. The cooperation observed in the integrated camp served competitive values.

To summarize, we found the condition of voluntary segregation to exhibit primarily cooperative behavior with little overt competitive behavior. In the integrated situation competitive behavior predominated, with much cooperative behavior seeming to serve the purpose of inter-group competition.

Is one form of social organization preferable over another? Is cooperation the ideal state, as Philip Slater proposes?

> Hence the only obstacle to utopia is the persistence of the competitive motivational patterns that past scarcity assumptions have spawned. Nothing stands in our way except our invidious dreams of personal glory. Our horror of group coercion reflects our reluctance

to relinquish these dreams although they have brought us nothing but misery, discontent, hatred, and chaos. If we can overcome this horror, however, and mute this vanity we may again be able to take up our original utopian tasks. (Slater, 1970, p 150)

In our view both competitive and cooperative behavior have positive and negative aspects. Competition is not merely due to dreams of personal glory, and a result of scarcity, but also serves other aims. For example, a means for a person to experience himself as separate from a group, or a means to be productive, creative, achieving. Thus, more than "misery, discontent, hatred and chaos" may result from competition.

As we indicated earlier in this chapter, cooperative behavior also has its limitations. It may, through excessive group dependence, prevent the fullest individual expression and self-development. To promote voluntary segregated social structures, generalizing from our observations, would be to promote cooperative behavior and effectively limit competitive behavior. On the other hand, integrated social conditions can be designed to promote both competitive and cooperative behavior, through manipulation of the social dynamics of subgroups or by emphasis on group rather than individual achievements.

Our conclusions would stress the importance and benefits of both structures for any individual, and to hope for the opportunity for him or her to move from one to another at any point in time depending on the fit, at that moment, between his needs and the effects to be expected in the different circumstances.

LIMITATIONS OF THE STUDY

In our discussion we have mentioned the possibility of generalizing our conclusions in terms of other conditions of deviant-majority relations. The limitations of the study suggest caution in generalizing before confirmatory research is done. A primary reason for caution is the complexity of the concept of deviance when applied to any "different" group. The deviance of the physically handicapped person is comparable only at a gross conceptual level to the deviance of women, the aged or the mentally ill in our society. A social psychological study of one group at best can be only suggestive in understanding the dynamics of the other groups.

Our sample of both camps and campers was small because of the nature of the subject, and because of the methods used. It took most of one summer to study only one segregated camp. Its representativeness of special camps in general had been established only by discussion with persons knowledgeable in the camping field. In the integrated camps only ten handicapped children could be followed in an entire summer because the camps only took five per session.

Some differences we have attributed to social structure were possibly due to different camp acceptance policies, different sexual ratios, or different leadership. It was found, for example, that relationships were deeper and closer in the segregated social system. While this could be due, in part, to the openness in self revelation, there was also a higher return rate at the special camp, resulting in more youngsters knowing each other from past years. A better design for the study, although more difficult to arrange, would be to use children as their own controls, following the same children in both integrated and segregated systems.

As to limitations of method, the depth of understanding of a social system gained through intensive field methods is at the expense of "hard" data, objectively measurable phenomena which are considered more generalizable evidence. In this study, field observations were supplemented by interviews and camp records. Yet conclusions are still limited by the influence of the researchers' perspective and interpretations.

Even though field observers are guided in their observations by theoretically derived foci of attention (what to note in the complexity of field setting and behavior), the richness of both the stream of events and each observer's unique orientation means that field studies yield rich but perhaps unique conclusions, inevitably hard to replicate by other investigators.

Further limitations of the study's generalizability to other situations of integration or segregation of deviant persons arise from the fact that children were studied, not adults, and that the situations of group living observed were short term (two to four weeks). One can think of many reasons why extrapolation of results and conclusions would be hazardous to the situation of adults, or group arrangements of longer or shorter duration.

Adult members of a deviant category, compared to children, would have longer experience with the social problems of being different. They would have more self-consistency and confirmed patterns of social behavior. Might their behavior, then, be different from that of children if put in time-limited groupings such as camps? Perhaps the effects of the different social structures would be less pronounced or slower in coming. For this reason, it was fortunate that we used children as subjects because children have a faster rate of adaptation to the effects of new situations and we were able to find effects of social structure on interaction in relatively brief periods of time.

If more permanent rather than time-limited social situations were studied, the effects of social structure on social interaction which we found may have been even more pronounced, but this is, of course, conjecture. Conversely, had briefer periods been studied, effects may have been less sharply defined with more individual and sub-group variability of behavior.

We must consider also that the present study focused on *physically* disabled children in a special setting, summer camps. By definition, camps stress the physical aspects of behavior. Did this special matching of deviant characteristics and the demands of the setting intensify some effects that were found? An analogy would be studying integration or segregation of aged persons in an educational setting. The older person's difficulties in new learning (Birren, 1959) would be matched by the demands of the setting. Different results might be found if physically handicapped children had been studied in school settings or if older persons were studied in integrated or segregated housing.

SOCIAL CHANGE

It has been pointed out in this study that both the integrated and segregated social structures have positive and negative aspects in terms of social interaction, the development of dependent or independent behavior, high productivity or low productivity, cooperative or competitive behavior.

It seems very possible that some aspects of both types of camp could be altered to some extent by changes in programming and orientation of staff. In integrated camps, perpetuation of denial or avoidance of physical disability was found to be detrimental to the development of close relationships and self-esteem. Defensive behavior would diminish if the staff, perhaps in group sessions, could be led to discuss openly their fears and prejudices about physical deviance and the benefits of open attention to these matters.

Programming might be based on principles of cooperation, as well as competition. Counselors could have training in how rules of play or work could be made flexible, adapted to individuals so that normal children would not be resentful of handicapped players at the same time the latter could participate with some feeling of confidence without slowing others down. Counselors could be taught the concepts of core and *para* roles, parallel play, and grouping children according to functional capacities. There could be greater emphasis given to non-physical activities, such as reading, singing, newspaper writing or dramatics. Some of the programming should be derived from the interests and concerns of the campers rather than being totally prearranged.

The dependency developed in the segregated camp, accompanied by a lower sense of responsibility or self-initiative might be altered by training of staff. Group discussions might be held so that counselors and staff could discuss how they might be unconsciously promoting dependency and depriving the children of opportunities to develop initiative. While there seems to be a high correlation between the type of social structure and the social interaction that occurs, there is also a high degree of potential for altering the social structure, thereby offering opportunities to influence social behavior.

REFERENCES

1. Birren, James E.: Handbook of Aging and the Individual. Chicago, University of Chicago Press, 1959.
2. Blackman, Leonard S. and Heintz, Paul: The mentally retarded. Review of Educational Research, 36:5, 1966.
3. Breslin, Hazel B.: The relationship between the physically handicapped child's self-concept and his peer reputation. Dissertation Abstracts, 1493, 1968.
4. Bruning, James L. and Kintz, B. L.: Computational Handbook of Statistics. Glenview, Ill.: Scott, Foresman, 1968.
5. Coopersmith, Stanley: The Antecedents of Self-esteem. San Francisco, W. H. Freeman, 1967.
6. Craig, Helen B.: A sociometric investigation of self-concept of the deaf child. American Annals of the Deaf, 110:456, 1965.
7. Davis, Fred: Deviance disavowal: the management of strained interaction by the visibly handicapped. In Manis, J. G. and Meltzer, B. N. (Eds.): Symbolic Interaction. Boston, Allyn and Bacon, 1967.
8. Dembo, Tamara; Leviton, Gloria and Wright, Beatrice A.: Adjustment to misfortune: a problem of social psychological rehabilitation. Artificial Limbs, 3:4, 1956.
9. Dibner, Andrew S. and Dibner, Susan S.: Report on Studies of Integrated Camping. Easter Seal Society of Massachusetts, Oct. 1968.
10. Dibner, Andrew S. and Dibner, Susan S.: Integration or segregation of deviants? The physically handicapped child. Community Mental Health Journal, 7:3, 1971.
11. Easter Seal Guide to Special Camping Programs. National Easter Seal Society for Crippled Children and Adults, 1968.
12. Flapan, Dorothy: Children's Understanding of Social Interaction. New York, Teachers College Press, Columbia University, 1968.
13. Freedman, Jonathan L. and Doob, Anthony N.: Deviancy: The Psychology of Being Different. New York, Academic Press, 1968.
14. Goffman, Erving: Stigma: Notes on the Management of Spoiled Identity. Englewood Cliffs, New Jersey, Prentice-Hall, 1963.
15. Hamilton, K. W.: Counseling the handicapped in the rehabilitation process. Quoted in Wright, Beatrice A.: Physical Disabilities: A Psychological Approach. New York Harper and Row, 1960, p. 9.
16. Krider, Mary Althea: Comparative studies of the self concepts of crippled and non-crippled children. Dissertation Abstracts, 20:2143, 1959.

17. Lipsitt, Lewis P.: A self-concept scale for children and its relationship to the children's form of the Manifest Anxiety Scale. Child Development, 29:463, 1968.
18. May, Rollo: The Meaning of Anxiety. New York, Ronald, 1950.
19. Meissner, Ann L.; Thoreson, Richard W. and Butler, A. J.: Relation of self concept to impact and obviousness of disability among male and female adolescents. Perceptual and Motor Skills, 24:1099, 1967.
20. Mussen, Paul H. and Barker, Roger G.: Attitudes toward cripples. Journal of Abnormal and Social Psychology, 39, 1944.
21. Richardson, Stephen A.; Hastorf, Albert H. and Dornbusch, Sanford M.: Effects of physical disability on a child's description of himself. Child Development, 35:894, 1964.
22. Scott, Robert A.: The Making of Blind Men: A Study of Adult Socialization. New York, Russell Sage Foundation, 1969.
23. Sherif, Muzafer; Harvey, O. J.; White, B. J.; Hood, W. R. and Sherif, C. W.: Intergroup Conflict and Cooperation: The Robbers Cave Experiment. Norman U. Book Exchange, 1961.
24. Slater, Philip E.: The Pursuit of Loneliness: American Culture at the Breaking Point. Boston, Beacon Press, 1970.
25. Smits, Stanley J.: Reactions of self and others to the obviousness and severity of physical disability. Dissertation Abstacts, 1324, 1964.
26. Webster's New Collegiate Dictionary, Springfield Mass., Merriam, 1961.
27. White, Robert W.: Motivation reconsidered: the concept of competence. Psychological Review. 66:297, 1959.
28. Wright, Beatrice A.: Physical Disability: A Psychological Approach. New York, Harper and Row, 1960.

Appendix I

INTERVIEW WITH COUNSELORS: INTEGRATED CAMPS

Note: Probe all open questions. Follow up spontaneous remarks.

A. Demographic

Name.

Address.

Age.

Education; College major.

Vocational Goals.

Father's occupation.

Who is in your family? Ages of siblings?

B. Work and Education

Have you ever worked before? Where?

How did you decide to be a counselor in a summer camp?

Previous counseling jobs. When? Where? If other camps, what were they like? What were the campers like?

Have you worked with handicapped children before?

Did you know any handicapped people before?

Do you have any handicaps?

C. Attitudes toward Campers and the Job

How would you describe your job at camp? What do you do?

What is the main purpose of a camp like this?

Do the children in your cabin make a good grouping?

Did you know that some children would be handicapped?

How do you feel about_____(H'c camper in cabin)?

Were you given special orientation or help in handling problems with the handicapped children? Should orientation be done differently?

Do the handicapped children take up extra time? How do you feel about it?

How does_____(H'c child) get along with other children and counselors? (Probe, ask for incidents).

How would you describe an ideal camper? Who comes closest to this? Why?

How would you describe a poor camper? Who comes closest to this? Why?

How do you think it works, having handicapped children in a regular camp like this? Should they be in special camps?

D. Problems at Work

What are the biggest problems you have as a counselor? How do you deal with them?

Is there anything about camp that you think could be improved? How?

Any questions that you want to ask me?

Appendix II

INTERVIEW WITH COUNSELORS: SEGREGATED CAMP

Note: Probe all open questions. Follow up spontaneous remarks.

A. Demographic (Same as for Integrated Camps, see above).

B. Work and Education (Same as for Integrated Camps, see above).

C. Attitudes Toward Campers and Job

How would you describe your job at camp? What do you do?

What is the main purpose of a camp like Woodland?

Do you think the children in your cabin make a good grouping?

Do you see the children as different from each other? How?

How would you describe an ideal camper? Which child in your cabin comes closest to this? Why?

How would you describe a poor camper? Who comes close to this? Why?

Which child do you admire most in camp? Why?

Who are the most disabled? Why?

Who in your cabin could go to a regular camp? Why?

How do you think it would be to have 10 or 12 normal

children in a cabin with 1 or 2 handicapped campers?

Would you take a job in a regular camp? Why? Why not?

What do you think of Woodland being co-educational?

D. Problems at Work (Same as for Integrated Camps, see above).

INTERVIEW WITH CAMPERS

Note: Probe on all questions.

A. Personal Information

Name;   Address.

Age.

Have you been to camp before? Where? When?

How many times?

Did you enjoy it?

Could you tell me who is in your family, and how old they are?

What does your father do?

Does your mother work? If so, what does she do?

Do you have your own room at home? If not who do you share it with?

Would you like to have one of your own if you don't?

Where do you go to school? Is it a special school? Are you in a special class?

B. Friendship Networks

Who are your friends? (If only names of those in cabin, ask

194

about others in camp).

Why?

Who do you like best? Why?

What's she (he) like?

Who do you think likes you best? Why?

Of all the kids in camp, which ones don't you like very much? Why?

Who do you like least? Why?

Who do you think likes you least? Why?

C. Attitudes toward Camp *School*

Do you like being in camp?

What do you like about camp?

Would you rather be doing something else rather than be here? What?

How could camp be better?

What are some camp rules?

Are there any you especially don't like?

Are there any restrictions about where you can go?

D. Feelings of Competence

What do you like to do? How good are you at it?

How do you know you are good (fair, poor etc.)?

How are you at _____(activity named above) compared to most kids your age?

What are you going to do in camp today? Tomorrow?

How do you think you'll do at _____(activity named above)?

How do you think the other kids will do?

How do you think your best friend will do?

Do you like arts and crafts (or other non-competitive activity)?

How do you do at it? How do you know you are (good, fair, poor)?

E. Self-Other

In what ways are you like the other children in the cabin?

Who in your group are you most like?

Who are you least like?

In what ways are you different from the other children in the cabin?

How would you describe yourself?

F. Counselors

Who is your counselor?

What is your counselor like?

What do you like about her (him)?

What don't you like about her (him)?

Does she (he) pay more attention to some kids than to others? To whom? Why?

How do you feel about that?

Would you like to be a counselor?

Who would you like to be like most in the entire camp? Why?

Who wouldn't you like to be like? Why?

(For handicapped children) I would like to know more about your handicap. Could you tell me about it?

INDEX

A

Age differences, 90, 128
Aged, 185
Agencies, 5
Aggressiveness, 175
Anxiety, 134
Architecture, 22, 31, 34, 71

B

Beauty contest, 121
Blind, 5, 27, 72

C

Campers
  adjustment, 13
  grouping, 62, 70, 75, 78
  interests, 70, 81, 118, 120
  participation of, 61, 108, 111
  social background, 28, 36
Camps
  descriptions, 14, 22, 30
  goals, 61, 134
  selection, 13, 14, 16, 20
Camperships, 24, 34
Colostomy, 91
Commitment to integration, 12, 57-60, 86, 109, 123
Commitment to segregation, 47, 48-52, 86
Comparison with others, 133
Competence, 134
Competition, 7, 8, 35, 73, 107
  value, 153, 156, 158, 170
Cooperation, 72, 88, 102-103, 163, 181-183
Core roles, 84-86
Counselors
  attitudes toward camp, 46

attitudes toward handicapped children, 39, 44-45, 54, 58, 65-68, 80, 83, 111, 122
attitudes toward normal children, 41, 44, 56, 58
attitudes toward work, 42, 43-44
background, 53
ratios, 41, 57
relationships with campers, 103, 108-113
training, 55, 186

D

Dance, 142, 150
Deaf, 119-154
Dependency, 5, 186
Deviance, 10
Disability, 9

E

Education, 6, 28, 170

F

Family, 7, 102
Field observations, 15
Friendships, 95, 97, 114, 139, 151
Functional ability, 23, 64, 77

G

Group discussions, 18
Grouping
  by functional ability, 64-68
  by interests, 70-78

H

Handicaps (*See* Physical handicaps)